PRAISE FOR ANDREW HINTON

From "AI Basics for Managers:"

"a beacon, guiding non-tech leaders through the often murky waters of artificial intelligence"

— KIRAN

"this book is your ticket to understanding AI's potential and implementing it effectively"

— KAM

"the book was written in an easy-to-understand style, with enough info to make it interesting and informational, but not too much technical data ... the futuristic images, nice touch and beautifully reflects the topic of the book"

— SHAMSA K

"book's holistic approach, ranging from AI's history to its potential impact on contemporary business, is truly commendable"

— AES

AI AND ML FOR CODERS

AI AND ML FOR CODERS

A COMPREHENSIVE GUIDE TO ARTIFICIAL
INTELLIGENCE AND MACHINE LEARNING
TECHNIQUES, TOOLS, REAL-WORLD
APPLICATIONS, AND ETHICAL CONSIDERATIONS
FOR MODERN PROGRAMMERS

AI FUNDAMENTALS

ANDREW HINTON

B

Book Bound
STUDIOS

To the relentless innovators and curious minds who code not just with their hands but their hearts, may this book fuel your passion and guide you through the thrilling landscape of AI and ML.

The question of whether a computer can think is no more interesting than the question of whether a submarine can swim.

— EDSGER DIJKSTRA

CONTENTS

Receive Your Free Copy of The Power of AI

Or visit:
bookboundstudios.wixsite.com/andrew-hinton

INTRODUCTION TO ARTIFICIAL INTELLIGENCE AND MACHINE LEARNING FOR CODERS

In the ever-evolving landscape of technology, artificial intelligence (AI) and machine learning (ML) have emerged as two of the most transformative forces shaping our world today. As we stand at the cusp of a new era, coders, developers, and enthusiasts must understand and harness the power of these groundbreaking technologies. This book, "AI and ML for Coders," aims to serve as a comprehensive guide, providing readers with the knowledge and tools necessary to navigate the fascinating world of AI and ML.

AI and ML are vast and diverse, encompassing various techniques, algorithms, and applications. From natural language processing and computer vision to predictive analytics and autonomous systems, the potential of AI and ML to revolutionize industries and improve our daily lives is immense. As a coder, you are uniquely positioned to contribute to this revolution, leveraging your skills and creativity to develop innovative solutions that can change the world.

In this introductory chapter, we will embark on a journey through the history and evolution of AI and ML, tracing their roots and exploring the milestones that have shaped their development. We will also discuss the purpose and scope of this book, highlighting the unique blend of theory, practice, and real-world applications that sets it apart from other resources in the field. Furthermore, we will delve into the author's perspective, offering insights into the experiences and expertise that have informed the creation of this comprehensive guide.

As we progress through the chapters, we will delve deeper into the intricacies of AI and ML, equipping you with the knowledge and skills necessary to implement these technologies in your projects. Whether you are a seasoned developer looking to expand your repertoire or a curious enthusiast eager to learn more about AI and ML, this book caters to your needs and interests.

So, let us embark on this transformative journey together as we unveil the world of AI and ML for coders and unlock the potential of these powerful technologies to shape the future of our world.

Tracing the Evolution of Artificial Intelligence and Machine Learning

The fascinating world of Artificial Intelligence (AI) and Machine Learning (ML) has come a long way since its inception. To truly appreciate the power and potential of these technologies, it is essential to understand their historical roots and the milestones that have shaped their development. In this section, we will embark on a captivating journey through time, tracing the evolution of AI and ML and highlighting the key moments that have defined their growth.

The concept of AI dates back to ancient times, with myths and legends featuring intelligent machines and automatons. However, the modern era of AI began in the mid-20th century, when British mathematician and computer scientist Alan Turing proposed the Turing Test in 1950. This test assessed a machine's ability to exhibit intelligent behavior indistinguishable from a human's. Turing's work laid the foundation for the field of AI, sparking the imagination of researchers and visionaries alike.

In 1956, the Dartmouth Conference marked the birth of AI as a formal academic discipline. This gathering of scientists and mathematicians aimed to explore the possibilities of creating machines capable of simulating human intelligence. Early AI research focused on symbolic reasoning and problem-solving, giving rise to the development of programming languages like LISP and Prolog.

The 1960s and 1970s saw the emergence of various AI techniques, including knowledge representation, natural language processing, and expert systems. These approaches aimed to replicate human expertise in specific domains, such as medical diagnosis or financial planning. However, the limitations of these early AI systems soon became apparent as they needed help to cope with the complexity and ambiguity of real-world problems.

The 1980s marked a turning point in the evolution of AI and ML with the advent of connectionism and neural networks. Inspired by the structure and function of the human brain, these models sought to emulate how neurons process and transmit information. The development of the backpropagation algorithm enabled the efficient training of neural networks, paving the way for the emergence of deep learning in the subsequent decades.

The 1990s and 2000s witnessed significant advancements in ML, fueled by the increasing availability of data and computational power. The introduction of support vector machines, decision trees, and ensemble methods expanded the ML toolkit, enabling the development of more sophisticated and accurate models. During this period, AI and ML began to permeate various industries, from finance and healthcare to entertainment and e-commerce.

The 2010s saw the rise of deep learning, a subset of ML that leverages neural networks with multiple layers to learn complex patterns and representations. Breakthroughs in image recognition, natural language processing, and reinforcement learning have propelled AI and ML to the forefront of technological innovation. Today, AI and ML are transforming how we live, work, and interact with applications ranging from self-driving cars and virtual assistants to medical diagnostics and personalized recommendations.

In conclusion, the evolution of AI and ML has been remarkable, marked by groundbreaking discoveries, innovative techniques, and visionary thinkers. As we delve deeper into the world of AI and ML for coders, it is crucial to appreciate the rich history that has shaped these technologies and their immense potential for the future.

Empowering Coders to Harness the Power of AI and ML

The dawn of the digital age has brought many technological advancements. Among these innovations, Artificial Intelligence (AI) and Machine Learning (ML) have emerged as game-changers in computing. As we delve deeper into the 21st century, the significance of AI and ML in shaping our lives and industries is becoming increasingly apparent. Consequently, the demand for skilled coders who can harness the power of these technologies is on the rise.

The primary purpose of this book is to empower coders like you to tap into the immense potential of AI and ML. By providing a comprehensive understanding of these technologies' fundamental concepts, techniques, and applications, this book aims to equip you with the knowledge and skills required to excel in the rapidly evolving landscape of AI and ML.

This book is designed to serve as a valuable resource for coders, developers, and enthusiasts who wish to explore the fascinating world of AI and ML. It offers a unique blend of theory, practice, and real-world applications, ensuring that you not only grasp the underlying principles of these technologies but also learn how to apply them effectively in various contexts.

As you progress through the chapters, you will be introduced to various AI and ML techniques, ranging from basic algorithms to advanced neural networks. Each topic is presented clearly and concisely, emphasizing practical examples and hands-on exercises that will enable you to implement your newfound knowledge.

Moreover, this book adopts an engaging and persuasive writing style, encouraging you to embrace the transformative power of AI and ML and inspiring you to become an active participant in the ongoing technological revolution. By the time you reach the final pages, you will have gained a solid foundation in AI and ML and the confidence to apply these technologies in your projects and contribute to the broader coding community.

In summary, this book aims to empower you, the coder, to harness the power of AI and ML and embark on a transformative journey into these cutting-edge technologies. By providing a comprehensive, practical, and engaging learning experience, this book aims to equip you with the tools and knowledge necessary to thrive in the exciting world of AI and ML. So, let us begin this adventure together and unlock the limitless possibilities that await us in the fascinating world of Artificial Intelligence and Machine Learning.

Exploring the Breadth and Depth of AI and ML Techniques

In this groundbreaking book, we will embark on an enlightening journey that delves into the vast and intricate world of Artificial Intelligence (AI) and Machine Learning (ML) for coders. Our expedition will traverse the expansive landscape of these revolutionary technologies, providing readers with a comprehensive understanding of their underlying principles, techniques, and applications.

To begin, we will explore the foundational concepts and theories that form the bedrock of AI and ML. This will include examining the various types of AI, such as narrow, general, and superintelligence, and the fundamental principles of ML, including supervised, unsupervised, and reinforcement learning. By establishing a solid theoretical base, coders will be well-equipped to appreciate the practical aspects of these technologies.

Next, we will delve into the heart of AI and ML techniques, dissecting the inner workings of popular algorithms and models. This will encompass various topics, from neural networks and deep learning to natural language processing and computer vision. By examining these techniques in detail, readers will gain a thorough understanding of the mechanics behind these powerful tools, enabling them to harness their full potential in coding projects.

As we venture further into AI and ML, we will also discuss these technologies' ethical considerations and potential pitfalls. This will include an analysis of the implications of AI and ML on privacy, security, and employment, as well as a discussion of the measures that can be taken to mitigate these concerns. By addressing these critical issues, we aim to foster a responsible and conscientious approach to developing and deploying AI and ML solutions.

In addition to providing a comprehensive overview of AI and ML techniques, this book will also showcase many real-world applications and case studies. These examples will span various industries and domains, such as healthcare, finance, and transportation, demonstrating the transformative impact of AI and ML on our everyday lives. By examining these practical applications, readers will gain valuable insights into how AI and ML can be harnessed to solve complex problems and drive innovation.

Finally, this book will cater to a diverse audience of coders, developers, and enthusiasts, regardless of their expertise in AI and ML. Through clear explanations, engaging examples, and practical exercises, we aim to make these cutting-edge technologies accessible and enjoyable for all readers. Whether you are a seasoned programmer seeking to expand your skillset or a curious enthusiast eager to explore the world of AI and ML, this book will serve as your indispensable guide on this transformative journey.

A Unique Blend of Theory, Practice, and Real-World Applications

I aim to provide readers with a comprehensive understanding of artificial intelligence (AI) and machine learning (ML) from a coder's perspective. This book is designed to be a unique blend of theory, practice, and real-world applications, ensuring that readers not only grasp the fundamental concepts but also learn how to apply them in their coding projects.

In the theoretical aspect of this book, I delve into the history and evolution of AI and ML, discussing the key milestones and breakthroughs that have shaped the field. This background information is crucial for coders to appreciate the significance of these technologies and their potential impact on the future of computing.

The practical component of the book focuses on the hands-on implementation of AI and ML techniques. Through step-by-step tutorials and examples, readers will learn how to build and train various models, such as neural networks, decision trees, and clustering algorithms. These practical exercises reinforce the theoretical concepts and provide coders with the necessary skills to integrate AI and ML into their projects.

Lastly, the real-world applications section showcases the versatility and potential of AI and ML across various industries, such as healthcare, finance, and transportation. By exploring case studies and success stories, readers will gain insights into how these technologies revolutionize our lives and work. This section also serves as a source of inspiration for coders, encouraging them to think creatively and develop innovative AI and ML solutions.

Throughout the book, I try to make complex concepts accessible to readers of all levels. I aim to demystify AI and ML, empowering coders to harness the power of these technologies and contribute to the ongoing advancements in the field.

In conclusion, this book offers a unique blend of theory, practice, and real-world applications, providing coders with a comprehensive understanding of AI and ML. By combining these elements, I aim to inspire and equip readers with the knowledge and skills to embark on their transformative journey into AI and ML.

Embarking on a Transformative Journey into the Realm of AI and ML

As we stand on the precipice of a new era in technology, the significance of artificial intelligence and machine learning cannot be overstated. These powerful tools have the potential to revolutionize industries, streamline processes, and, ultimately, improve the quality of life for people around the world. For coders, developers, and enthusiasts alike, the opportunity to harness AI and ML's power is exciting and transformative.

In this book, we have endeavored to provide a comprehensive and accessible introduction to the world of AI and ML for coders. By tracing the evolution of these technologies, exploring their breadth and depth, and offering a unique blend of theory, practice, and real-world applications, we aim to empower our readers to take full advantage of the opportunities that AI and ML present.

As you embark on this transformative journey, it is essential to remember that the field of AI and ML is vast and ever-evolving. As such, it is crucial to approach your studies with an open mind, a willingness to learn, and a commitment to staying current with the latest developments and advancements. By doing so, you will be well-equipped to navigate the complexities of AI and ML and ultimately make a meaningful impact in your chosen field.

In conclusion, we invite you to join us on this exciting adventure into artificial intelligence and machine learning. As you delve into this book's pages, we hope you will find inspiration, knowledge, and the tools necessary to participate actively in the AI and ML revolution. Together, let us explore the limitless possibilities these technologies offer and work towards a brighter, more efficient, and more connected future.

1

FOUNDATIONS OF AI: HISTORY, CONCEPTS, AND TERMINOLOGY

In recent years, artificial intelligence (AI) and machine learning (ML) fields have experienced a meteoric rise in popularity and application. These cutting-edge technologies have permeated nearly every aspect of our lives, from how we communicate and consume information to how we work and make decisions. As a coder, it is essential to understand the foundations of AI and ML, as they have become integral components of modern software development and innovation.

This chapter aims to provide a comprehensive overview of the history, core concepts, techniques, and terminology associated with AI and ML. By gaining a solid understanding of these topics, coders will be better equipped to harness the power of these technologies and stay ahead in the ever-evolving programming world.

The journey begins with a brief history of artificial intelligence, tracing its roots from the early days of computer science to the present day. This section will highlight key milestones and visionaries who have shaped the field, providing context for the development of AI and ML.

Next, we delve into the core concepts of AI, exploring the building blocks that underpin this fascinating field. From algorithms and heuristics to neural networks and natural language processing, this section will provide a solid foundation for understanding the inner workings of AI systems.

The focus then shifts to machine learning, a subset of AI that has garnered significant attention in recent years. This section will explore various techniques and applications of ML, demonstrating how coders can leverage these methods to create intelligent, adaptive software solutions.

A comprehensive glossary of essential terminology will be provided to ensure that readers are well-versed in the language of AI and ML. This vocabulary will serve as a valuable reference for coders navigating the complex landscape of AI and ML technologies.

Finally, the chapter will conclude with a look toward the future, examining the potential impact of AI and ML on the coding profession and beyond. As these technologies continue to advance rapidly, coders must stay informed and adapt to the changing landscape.

In summary, this chapter thoroughly introduces the world of AI and ML, equipping coders with the knowledge and tools necessary to excel in this exciting and dynamic field. By understanding the history, concepts, techniques, and terminology associated with AI and ML, coders will be well-prepared to harness the power of these technologies and shape the future of software development.

A Brief History of Artificial Intelligence: From Turing to Today

The fascinating journey of artificial intelligence (AI) and machine learning (ML) has its roots in the early 20th century, with the ground-breaking work of British mathematician and computer scientist Alan Turing. In this section, we will explore the milestones that have shaped the development of AI and ML and how they have become indispensable tools for coders in the modern world.

The Turing Test: The Birth of AI

In 1950, Alan Turing proposed a test to determine whether a machine could exhibit intelligent behavior indistinguishable from a human's. This test, known as the Turing Test, laid the foundation for AI. Turing's work sparked a wave of interest in the possibility of creating intelligent machines, and researchers began to explore the potential of computers to mimic human thought processes.

The Dartmouth Conference: Defining AI

In 1956, a group of scientists and mathematicians gathered at Dartmouth College to discuss the future of AI. This conference marked the birth of AI as a formal academic discipline. The attendees, including John McCarthy, Marvin Minsky, and Claude Shannon, defined AI as the science of creating machines that can perform tasks requiring human intelligence. This definition set the stage for decades of research and development in the field.

Early AI Programs: Exploring the Possibilities

Throughout the 1960s and 1970s, researchers developed several early AI programs that demonstrated the potential of computers to perform tasks such as problem-solving, language understanding, and learning. Some notable examples include:

- **General Problem Solver (GPS):** Developed by Allen Newell and Herbert A. Simon, GPS was an early AI program designed to imitate human problem-solving strategies.
- **ELIZA:** Created by Joseph Weizenbaum, ELIZA was a natural language processing program that could simulate conversations with humans.
- **SHRDLU:** Developed by Terry Winograd, SHRDLU was a program that could understand and manipulate objects in a virtual world using natural language commands.

The Rise of Machine Learning

In the 1980s, researchers focused on developing algorithms that could learn from data, giving birth to machine learning. This shift was driven by the realization that teaching machines to learn from data was more efficient than programming them explicitly. Key developments during this period include:

- **Decision Trees:** Ross Quinlan's development of the ID3 algorithm for generating decision trees marked a significant milestone in ML research.
- **Neural Networks:** Inspired by the human brain, researchers developed artificial neural networks that could learn to recognize patterns in data.
- **Reinforcement Learning:** Richard Sutton and Andrew Barto pioneered the field of reinforcement learning, where algorithms learn by interacting with their environment and receiving feedback.

The AI and ML Renaissance: Deep Learning and Beyond

The 21st century has seen an explosion of interest in AI and ML, fueled by advances in computing power, large datasets' availability, and algorithm design breakthroughs. The development of deep learning, a subset of ML that involves training large neural networks, has led to significant progress in areas such as image and speech recognition, natural language processing, and game-playing. Today, AI and ML are integral components of the coding world, with applications ranging from web development and data analysis to robotics and autonomous vehicles.

In conclusion, the history of AI and ML is a testament to the ingenuity and perseverance of researchers who have sought to understand and replicate human intelligence. As we continue to push the boundaries of what machines can do, the future of AI and ML promises to be an exciting and transformative journey for coders and society.

Core Concepts in AI: Understanding the Building Blocks

As we delve into the fascinating world of artificial intelligence (AI) and machine learning (ML), coders must grasp the fundamental concepts that underpin these technologies. In this section, we will explore the core building blocks of AI, providing you with a solid foundation to better understand and utilize these powerful tools in your coding projects.

Intelligent Agents

At the heart of AI lies the concept of an intelligent agent. An intelligent agent is a system that perceives its environment, processes the gathered information, and takes appropriate actions to achieve specific goals. These agents can range from simple rule-based systems to complex neural networks capable of learning and adapting to their surroundings.

Problem Solving and Search

One of the primary tasks of AI is to solve problems. To accomplish this, AI systems employ various search algorithms to explore the solution space and identify the most suitable solution. These algorithms can be classified into two categories: uninformed search, which blindly explores the solution space, and informed search, which uses heuristics or other knowledge to guide the search process.

Knowledge Representation and Reasoning

Knowledge representation is the process of encoding information about the world in a form that an AI system can understand and manipulate. This can be achieved through various methods, such as propositional logic, first-order logic, semantic networks, and ontologies. Reasoning, on the other hand, is the process of concluding the represented knowledge. AI systems use deduction, induction, and abduction techniques to reason about the world and make decisions.

Machine Learning

Machine learning is a subset of AI that focuses on developing algorithms that enable computers to learn from and make predictions or decisions based on data. There are three main types of machine learning: supervised learning, where the algorithm is trained on a labeled dataset; unsupervised learning, where the algorithm learns patterns from an unlabeled dataset; and reinforcement learning, where the algorithm learns by interacting with its environment and receiving feedback in the form of rewards or penalties.

Neural Networks and Deep Learning

Neural networks are a machine learning model inspired by the structure and function of the human brain. These networks consist of interconnected nodes or neurons, which process and transmit information. Deep learning is a subset of neural networks that deal with large, complex models containing multiple layers of neurons. These deep neural networks have been instrumental in achieving breakthroughs in various AI applications, such as image recognition, natural language processing, and game playing.

Natural Language Processing

Natural language processing (NLP) is a branch of AI that focuses on enabling computers to understand, interpret, and generate human language. This involves speech recognition, sentiment analysis, machine translation, and text summarization. NLP techniques rely on machine learning algorithms and linguistic knowledge to process and analyze textual data.

By understanding these core concepts, you are now better equipped to appreciate the intricacies of AI and ML and their applications in the coding world. As we continue our journey, we will delve deeper into the techniques and applications of machine learning, providing you with the knowledge and tools to harness the power of AI in your coding projects.

Decoding Machine Learning: Techniques and Applications for Coders

As we delve deeper into artificial intelligence (AI), coders must understand the intricacies of machine learning (ML) – a subset of AI that focuses on developing algorithms and models that enable computers to learn and improve from experience. In this section, we will explore various ML techniques and their applications, providing you with the necessary knowledge to harness the power of AI in your coding projects.

Supervised Learning

Supervised learning is the most common ML technique, where the algorithm is trained on a labeled dataset, meaning that each data point has a corresponding output or label. Supervised learning aims to create a model that can make accurate predictions when presented with new, unseen data. This technique is widely used in applications such as image recognition, speech recognition, and natural language processing.

Some popular supervised learning algorithms include:

- **Linear Regression:** Used for predicting continuous values, such as house prices, based on various features like the number of rooms, location, and size.
- **Logistic Regression:** Used for binary classification problems, such as determining whether an email is spam.
- **Support Vector Machines (SVM):** A robust algorithm for classification and regression tasks, often used in image classification and handwriting recognition.
- **Decision Trees and Random Forests:** These algorithms are used for classification and regression tasks and are particularly useful for handling large datasets with multiple features.

Unsupervised Learning

In unsupervised learning, the algorithm is trained on an unlabeled dataset, meaning the data points do not have corresponding outputs or labels. Unsupervised learning aims to identify patterns or structures within the data, such as clustering or dimensionality reduction. This technique is often used for anomaly detection, data compression, and recommendation systems.

Some popular unsupervised learning algorithms include:

- **K-means Clustering:** A widely-used clustering algorithm that groups data points based on their similarity, often used for customer segmentation or image compression.
- **Principal Component Analysis (PCA):** A dimensionality reduction technique that transforms data into a lower-dimensional space, preserving as much information as

possible. PCA is often used for data visualization and noise reduction.

Reinforcement Learning

Reinforcement learning is an ML technique where an agent learns to make decisions by interacting with its environment and receiving feedback as rewards or penalties. Reinforcement learning aims to train the agent to make the best possible decisions to maximize its cumulative reward. This technique is commonly used in robotics, game-playing, and autonomous vehicles.

Some popular reinforcement learning algorithms include:

- **Q-Learning:** A model-free algorithm that learns an action-value function, which estimates the expected reward for a specific action in a given state.
- **Deep Q-Network (DQN):** A combination of Q-learning and deep neural networks, DQN has achieved human-level performance in playing Atari games.

In conclusion, understanding the various machine learning techniques and their applications is essential for coders looking to harness the power of AI. Mastering these concepts will enable you to tackle various coding projects, from building intelligent chatbots to developing self-driving cars. As AI and ML continue to evolve, the possibilities for their integration into the coding world are virtually limitless, making it an exciting time to be a coder.

AI and ML Terminology: Essential Vocabulary for the Modern Coder

As we delve deeper into artificial intelligence (AI) and machine learning (ML), coders must familiarize themselves with the essential vocabulary that defines these fields. This section aims to provide a comprehensive overview of the key terms and concepts that every modern coder should know. By mastering this terminology, you will be better equipped to understand and navigate the ever-evolving landscape of AI and ML.

- **Artificial Intelligence (AI):** AI refers to developing computer systems that can perform tasks that typically require human intelligence. These tasks include learning, reasoning, problem-solving, perception, and natural language understanding.
- **Machine Learning (ML):** ML is a subset of AI that focuses on developing algorithms and statistical models that enable computers to learn and improve from experience without being explicitly programmed. In other words, ML allows computers to adapt and make decisions based on data input automatically.
- **Deep Learning:** Deep learning is a subfield of ML that uses artificial neural networks to model and solve complex problems. These networks are designed to mimic the structure and function of the human brain, allowing computers to process and analyze vast amounts of data with remarkable accuracy.
- **Supervised Learning:** Supervised learning is a type of ML where the algorithm is trained on a labeled dataset containing input data and the corresponding correct output. Supervised learning aims to develop a model that can accurately predict the output for new, unseen data.
- **Unsupervised Learning:** Unlike supervised learning, unsupervised learning involves training an algorithm on an unlabeled dataset, where the input data does not have a corresponding output. Unsupervised learning aims to identify patterns, relationships, or structures within the data.
- **Reinforcement Learning:** Reinforcement learning is a type of ML where an agent learns to make decisions by interacting with its environment and receiving feedback

through rewards or penalties. Reinforcement learning aims to develop a policy that maximizes the cumulative reward over time.

- **Neural Network**: A neural network is a computational model inspired by the structure and function of the human brain. It consists of interconnected nodes, or neurons, that process and transmit information. Neural networks are the foundation of deep learning and are used to model complex patterns and relationships in data.
- **Algorithm**: An algorithm is a step-by-step procedure for solving or performing a problem. In AI and ML, algorithms process data, make decisions, and generate predictions or recommendations.
- **Feature**: A feature is an individual measurable property or characteristic of an observed phenomenon. In ML, features are input variables to train and test algorithms.
- **Model**: In ML, a model is a mathematical representation of a real-world process or system. Models are developed using algorithms and are trained on data to make predictions or decisions.

By understanding and incorporating these essential AI and ML terms into your coding vocabulary, you will be better prepared to tackle the challenges and opportunities that lie ahead in this rapidly evolving field. As you continue to explore the foundations of AI and ML, remember that the key to success lies in your ability to adapt, learn, and grow alongside these transformative technologies.

The Future of AI and ML in Coding and Beyond

As we have journeyed through the fascinating world of artificial intelligence (AI) and machine learning (ML), it is evident that these technologies have become an integral part of the coding landscape. From their humble beginnings with Turing's groundbreaking work to the sophisticated algorithms that power today's most advanced applications, AI and ML have come a long way. As we look towards the future, it is essential to consider the potential impact of these technologies on the coding profession and the world at large.

The rapid advancements in AI and ML have opened up many opportunities for coders. With the increasing demand for AI-powered solutions across various industries, there is a growing need for skilled professionals who can develop and implement these technologies. As a result, coders who are well-versed in AI and ML concepts and techniques are likely to be in high demand in the coming years. By staying up-to-date with the latest developments and honing their skills in these areas, coders can position themselves at the forefront of this technological revolution.

Moreover, the integration of AI and ML into coding practices has the potential to transform the way we approach problem-solving and software development. By leveraging the power of these technologies, coders can create more efficient, accurate, and intelligent applications that can adapt and learn from their environments. This can lead to the development of innovative solutions that can tackle complex challenges and improve the overall quality of life.

However, it is crucial to recognize that the widespread adoption of AI and ML also raises several ethical and societal concerns. Data privacy, algorithmic bias, and the potential displacement of human workers by automation are just a few of the challenges that need to be addressed as we continue to integrate these technologies into our daily lives. As responsible professionals, coders must be aware of these concerns and strive to develop AI and ML solutions that are transparent, fair, and beneficial to all.

In conclusion, the future of AI and ML in coding is undoubtedly promising, with immense potential for growth and innovation. As we continue to explore the capabilities of these technologies, it is up to us, the coders, to harness their power responsibly and ethically. By doing so, we can help shape a future where AI and ML not only revolutionize the coding profession but also contribute to the betterment of society.

Chapter Summary

- AI and ML have experienced a rapid rise in popularity and application, becoming integral components of modern software development and innovation.
- The history of AI and ML can be traced back to the early 20th century, with key milestones and visionaries shaping the field, such as Alan Turing and the Dartmouth Conference.
- Core concepts in AI include intelligent agents, problem-solving and search, knowledge representation and reasoning, machine learning, neural networks and deep learning, and natural language processing.
- Machine learning techniques can be classified into supervised, unsupervised, and reinforcement learning, each with its own algorithms and applications.
- Deep learning, a subset of ML, involves training large neural networks and has led to significant progress in areas such as image and speech recognition, natural language processing, and game-playing.
- Familiarity with essential AI and ML terminology, such as supervised learning, unsupervised learning, reinforcement learning, and neural networks, is crucial for modern coders.
- The future of AI and ML in coding is promising, with immense potential for growth, innovation, and the development of intelligent, adaptive software solutions.
- Ethical and societal concerns, such as data privacy, algorithmic bias, and the potential displacement of human workers, must be addressed as AI and ML technologies continue to advance and integrate into our daily lives.

2

MACHINE LEARNING BASICS: SUPERVISED, UNSUPERVISED, AND REINFORCEMENT LEARNING

I n the 21st century, artificial intelligence (AI) and machine learning (ML) have emerged as powerful tools transforming how we approach problem-solving and decision-making. As a coder, harnessing the potential of AI and ML can significantly enhance your capabilities and open up a world of possibilities. In this chapter, we will delve into the fascinating realm of machine learning, exploring its core concepts and techniques, and providing you with a solid foundation to incorporate these cutting-edge technologies into your coding repertoire.

At its core, machine learning is a subset of artificial intelligence that focuses on the development of algorithms and models that enable computers to learn and adapt from experience without being explicitly programmed. This ability to learn from data and improve over time allows machine learning systems to make predictions, identify patterns, and optimize processes with minimal human intervention.

There are three primary types of machine learning: supervised learning, unsupervised learning, and reinforcement learning. Each approach offers unique advantages and is suited to different types of problems and datasets. In the following sections, we will examine these learning methods in detail, providing a comprehensive understanding of their underlying principles, applications, and limitations.

As we embark on this journey through machine learning, it is essential to remember that the true power of AI and ML lies in their ability to augment human intelligence and creativity. By mastering these techniques and incorporating them into your coding projects, you will be well-equipped to tackle complex challenges, drive innovation, and shape the future of technology. So, let us begin our exploration of machine learning basics and unlock the potential of AI and ML for coders.

Supervised Learning: Training with Labeled Data

In the fascinating world of artificial intelligence and machine learning, supervised learning is one of the most widely used and practical techniques. As coders, it is essential to understand the fundamentals of supervised learning to harness its full potential in your projects. In this section, we will delve into the concept of supervised learning, explore its applications, and discuss the steps involved in training a model using labeled data.

The Concept of Supervised Learning

Supervised learning is a type of machine learning where the algorithm is trained on a dataset containing input-output pairs, also known as labeled data. In other words, the algorithm learns from examples annotated with the correct output, allowing it to make predictions or decisions based on new, unseen data. The primary goal of supervised learning is to create a model that can generalize well to new instances, minimizing the error between the predicted and actual outputs.

Applications of Supervised Learning

The versatility of supervised learning has led to its widespread use across various domains. Some typical applications include:

- **Image recognition:** Identifying objects, people, or scenes in images.
- **Spam detection:** Filtering out unwanted emails based on their content.
- **Fraud detection:** Identifying suspicious activities in financial transactions.
- **Medical diagnosis:** Predicting the presence or absence of a disease based on patient data.
- **Language translation:** Converting text from one language to another.

Training a Model with Labeled Data

The process of training a supervised learning model involves several crucial steps. Let's take a closer look at each of these steps:

- **Data collection and preprocessing:** The first step is to gather a dataset containing input-output pairs. This dataset must be large and diverse enough to represent the problem space accurately. The data may need to be cleaned, normalized, or transformed to ensure the algorithm can process it efficiently.

- **Model selection:** Next, you must choose an appropriate machine learning algorithm based on the problem. Some popular supervised learning algorithms include linear regression, logistic regression, support vector machines, and neural networks.
- **Model training:** The chosen algorithm is then trained on the labeled dataset. During this phase, the algorithm adjusts its parameters to minimize errors between its predictions and outputs. This process is often iterative, with the model improving its performance over multiple passes through the data.
- **Model evaluation:** Once the model has been trained, it is essential to evaluate its performance on a separate dataset that it has not seen before. This step helps to determine the model's ability to generalize to new instances. Standard evaluation metrics include accuracy, precision, recall, and F1 score.
- **Model tuning and optimization:** If the model's performance is unsatisfactory, you may need to fine-tune its parameters or optimize the algorithm to achieve better results. This process may involve adjusting the learning rate, changing the model's complexity, or employing regularization techniques to prevent overfitting.

In conclusion, supervised learning is a powerful and versatile technique that allows coders to create intelligent applications capable of making predictions and decisions based on labeled data. By understanding the fundamentals of supervised learning and following the steps outlined in this section, you can harness the power of AI and ML to enhance your coding projects and quickly solve complex problems.

Unsupervised Learning: Discovering Hidden Patterns

As we delve deeper into artificial intelligence and machine learning, it is essential to understand the different learning methods employed to solve various problems. In this section, we will explore the fascinating realm of unsupervised learning. This technique allows machines to discover hidden patterns and structures within data without prior guidance or labeled information.

The Essence of Unsupervised Learning

Imagine a scenario where you are presented with a large dataset containing information about various fruits. In supervised learning, you would have been provided with labeled data, such as the fruit's name, color, and size. However, in unsupervised learning, you are given no such labels. Your task is identifying any underlying patterns or structures within the data, such as clustering similar fruits or finding relationships between their attributes.

Unsupervised learning is a powerful technique that can be applied to various problems, from customer segmentation in marketing to anomaly detection in cybersecurity. By allowing machines to learn from unlabeled data, unsupervised learning opens up possibilities for discovering new insights and understanding complex systems.

Key Techniques in Unsupervised Learning

Several techniques in unsupervised learning can be employed to uncover hidden patterns within data. Two of the most common methods are clustering and dimensionality reduction.

Clustering involves grouping data points based on their similarity or proximity. Clustering algorithms, such as K-means or hierarchical clustering, can identify natural groupings within the data, which can be analyzed further to reveal insights or inform decision-making processes.

High-dimensional data can be challenging to analyze and visualize. Dimensionality reduction techniques, such as Principal Component Analysis (PCA) or t-Distributed Stochastic Neighbor Embedding (t-SNE), aim to reduce the number of dimensions in the data while preserving its essential structure. This can reveal hidden patterns and simplify the analysis process.

Advantages and Limitations of Unsupervised Learning

Unsupervised learning offers several advantages over supervised learning, such as the ability to work with unlabeled data and the potential to uncover previously unknown patterns or relationships. However, it also comes with its own set of challenges and limitations.

One of the primary advantages of unsupervised learning is its ability to work with large volumes of unlabeled data. Obtaining labeled data can be time-consuming, expensive, or even impossible in many real-world scenarios. Unsupervised learning offers a solution to this problem by allowing machines to learn from the data without explicit guidance.

On the other hand, unsupervised learning can be more challenging to evaluate and interpret than supervised learning. Since there are no predefined labels or ground truth to compare the results against, it can be challenging to determine the accuracy or effectiveness of the model. Additionally, the lack of guidance can sometimes lead to unexpected or irrelevant patterns being discovered, which may not be helpful for the problem at hand.

In conclusion, unsupervised learning is a powerful and versatile technique that can be used to discover hidden patterns and structures within data. By understanding its key techniques, advantages, and limitations, coders can harness the power of AI and machine learning to tackle a wide range of problems and uncover new insights. As we continue exploring the world of AI and ML, it is essential to recognize the value of unsupervised learning and its potential to transform how we analyze and understand complex systems.

Reinforcement Learning: Learning through Interaction

As we delve deeper into the fascinating world of machine learning, we must explore the concept of reinforcement learning. This unique and powerful approach enables machines to learn through interaction. This section will discuss the fundamentals of reinforcement learning, its applications, and how it differs from supervised and unsupervised learning. By understanding the intricacies of reinforcement learning, coders can harness its potential to create intelligent systems that adapt and improve over time.

The Essence of Reinforcement Learning

Reinforcement learning is an area of machine learning that focuses on training algorithms to make decisions based on their interactions with an environment. In this learning paradigm, an agent (the learning algorithm) takes actions within a given environment to achieve a specific goal. The agent receives feedback through rewards or penalties, which it uses to adjust its behavior and improve its decision-making capabilities.

The primary objective of reinforcement learning is to enable the agent to learn an optimal policy, a set of rules that dictate the best course of action in any given situation. The agent's goal is to maximize the cumulative reward it receives over time, which requires striking a balance between exploration (trying new actions) and exploitation (choosing the best-known action).

Key Components of Reinforcement Learning

Reinforcement learning comprises several essential components, including:

- **Agent:** The learning algorithm that interacts with the environment and makes decisions.
- **Environment:** The context in which the agent operates and takes actions.
- **State:** A representation of the current situation within the environment.

- **Action:** A decision made by the agent that affects the environment.
- **Reward:** Feedback provided to the agent based on the consequences of its actions.

These components work together in a cyclical process, with the agent continually observing the environment, taking actions, receiving rewards, and updating its knowledge to improve future decision-making.

Applications of Reinforcement Learning

Reinforcement learning has applications in various fields, including robotics, finance, healthcare, and gaming. Some notable examples include:

- **Robotics:** Reinforcement learning algorithms have been used to teach robots to walk, grasp objects, and navigate complex environments.
- **Finance:** In the financial sector, reinforcement learning has been employed to optimize trading strategies and manage investment portfolios.
- **Healthcare:** Reinforcement learning has been applied to personalize treatment plans for patients with chronic conditions, such as diabetes and cancer.
- **Gaming:** Reinforcement learning has trained AI agents to defeat human players in games like Go, chess, and poker.

Reinforcement Learning vs. Supervised and Unsupervised Learning

Reinforcement learning differs from supervised and unsupervised learning in several key aspects:

- **Feedback:** While supervised learning relies on labeled data to provide explicit feedback, reinforcement learning uses rewards and penalties as indirect feedback based on the agent's actions.

- **Exploration vs. Exploitation:** Reinforcement learning requires the agent to balance exploration and exploitation, a challenge not present in supervised or unsupervised learning.
- **Decision-making:** Reinforcement learning focuses on training agents to make decisions, whereas supervised and unsupervised learning primarily involves pattern recognition and data analysis.

In conclusion, reinforcement learning offers a dynamic and interactive approach to machine learning that empowers coders to create intelligent systems capable of learning from their experiences. By understanding the principles of reinforcement learning and its differences from supervised and unsupervised learning, coders can choose the most suitable learning method for their projects and harness the full potential of AI and ML in their work.

Comparing and Choosing the Right Learning Method

As we delve deeper into the world of artificial intelligence and machine learning, it becomes increasingly important to understand the distinctions between the various learning methods and how to choose the right one for your coding project. In this section, we will compare supervised, unsupervised, and reinforcement learning, highlight their strengths and weaknesses, and guide you in selecting the most suitable approach for your needs.

Supervised Learning: Training with Labeled Data

Strengths: Supervised learning is the most common and widely used method in machine learning. It excels in situations with a clear relationship between input and output data, and labeled data is readily available. This method is particularly effective for classification, regression, and prediction tasks.

Weaknesses: The primary drawback of supervised learning is its reliance on labeled data. Obtaining and maintaining a large dataset with accurate labels can be time-consuming and expensive. Additionally, supervised learning models may struggle with generalizing to new, unseen data if the training data needs to be more diverse.

When to choose: Opt for supervised learning when you have a well-defined problem with a clear input-output relationship and access to a substantial amount of labeled data.

Unsupervised Learning: Discovering Hidden Patterns

Strengths: Unsupervised learning shines when labeled data is scarce or nonexistent. It is adept at uncovering hidden patterns, structures, and relationships within the data, making it ideal for clustering, dimensionality reduction, and anomaly detection tasks.

Weaknesses: The primary limitation of unsupervised learning is its need for more precise, interpretable results. Since it does not rely on labeled data, the output may be challenging to understand and validate. Additionally, unsupervised learning models may require more computational resources and time to process large datasets.

When to choose: Choose unsupervised learning when you have a large amount of unlabeled data and are interested in discovering underlying patterns or structures within the data.

Reinforcement Learning: Learning through Interaction

Strengths: Reinforcement learning is particularly well-suited for problems involving decision-making and interacting with an environment. Through trial and error, it can learn optimal strategies and actions, making it ideal for game playing, robotics, and autonomous systems.

Weaknesses: Reinforcement learning can be computationally expensive and may require significant time to converge on an optimal solution. Additionally, it can be challenging to design an appropriate reward function that effectively guides the learning process.

When to choose: Opt for reinforcement learning when working on a problem involving sequential decision-making and interaction with an environment, and you are willing to invest time and resources in fine-tuning the learning process.

In conclusion, the choice of learning method depends on the nature of your problem, the availability of labeled data, and the desired outcome. By understanding the strengths and weaknesses of supervised, unsupervised, and reinforcement learning, you can make an informed decision and harness the power of AI and ML to elevate your coding projects to new heights.

Embracing the Power of AI and ML in Coding

As we reach the end of our journey through the fascinating world of artificial intelligence and machine learning, it is essential to take a moment to reflect on the immense potential these technologies hold for coders. By understanding the basics of machine learning, including supervised, unsupervised, and reinforcement learning, we have unlocked the door to a new realm of possibilities in the coding field.

The power of AI and ML lies in their ability to transform how we approach problem-solving and decision-making. By harnessing these technologies, coders can create more efficient, intelligent, and adaptable software solutions that can learn and grow over time. This enhances the user experience and allows developers to tackle increasingly complex challenges with greater ease and precision.

In today's rapidly evolving digital landscape, coders must stay ahead of the curve and embrace the latest advancements in AI and ML. By doing so, they can unlock new opportunities for innovation and growth, personally and professionally. As we have seen throughout this chapter, the key to success in this endeavor lies in understanding the fundamental principles of machine learning and selecting the most appropriate method for each unique situation.

As you continue to explore the world of AI and ML, remember that the journey does not end here. Machine learning constantly evolves, with new techniques and algorithms being developed daily. As a coder, it is up to you to stay informed and adapt to these changes, ensuring that your skills remain relevant and valuable in the ever-changing world of technology.

In conclusion, the power of AI and ML in coding cannot be over-stated. By embracing and incorporating these technologies into your work, you can unlock a world of possibilities and take your coding skills to new heights. So, go forth and harness the power of machine learning, and let it guide you on your path to becoming a more skilled, innovative, and successful coder.

Chapter Summary

- Machine learning, a subset of artificial intelligence, focuses on developing algorithms and models that enable computers to learn and adapt from experience without explicit programming.
- There are three primary types of machine learning: supervised learning (training with labeled data), unsupervised learning (discovering hidden patterns), and reinforcement learning (learning through interaction).
- Supervised learning is the most common method and is effective for classification, regression, and prediction tasks. It requires a large amount of labeled data and a clear input-output relationship.
- Unsupervised learning is ideal for uncovering hidden patterns and structures within data, especially when labeled data is scarce. It is suitable for clustering, dimensionality reduction, and anomaly detection tasks.
- Reinforcement learning is well-suited for problems involving decision-making and interaction with an environment. It is ideal for game-playing, robotics, and autonomous systems.

- Choosing the right learning method depends on the nature of the problem, the availability of labeled data, and the desired outcome. Understanding the strengths and weaknesses of each method is crucial for making an informed decision.
- The power of AI and ML lies in their ability to transform problem-solving and decision-making, allowing coders to create more efficient, intelligent, and adaptable software solutions.
- Staying informed and adapting to the constantly evolving field of machine learning is essential for coders to remain relevant and valuable in the ever-changing world of technology.

.

3

ESSENTIAL TOOLS AND LIBRARIES FOR AI AND ML DEVELOPMENT

I n the always-adapting world of artificial intelligence (AI) and machine learning (ML), developers constantly seek ways to create more efficient, accurate, and intelligent systems. To achieve this, they rely on a wide array of tools and libraries that simplify the development process and enhance the capabilities of their AI and ML projects. This chapter aims to provide an overview of the essential tools and libraries that every AI and ML developer should be familiar with, regardless of their level of expertise.

As we delve into AI and ML development, we must understand that these technologies are not limited to a single programming language or platform. Instead, they encompass various languages, libraries, and tools that cater to different needs and preferences. By exploring these options, developers can decide which tools best suit their projects and goals.

In the following sections, we will discuss popular programming languages for AI and ML and the most widely used machine learning libraries and frameworks. We will also explore deep learning libraries and tools, which have gained significant traction in recent years due to their ability to process vast amounts of data and generate highly accurate models. Finally, we will examine data visualization and analysis tools, which are essential for understanding and interpreting the results of AI and ML algorithms.

By the end of this chapter, you will have a solid understanding of the various tools and libraries available for AI and ML development, enabling you to choose the right ones for your projects and ultimately create more effective and intelligent systems. So, let's embark on this exciting journey and discover the essential tools and libraries that will empower you to harness the full potential of AI and ML technologies.

Popular Programming Languages for AI and ML

As we delve into the fascinating world of artificial intelligence (AI) and machine learning (ML), it is crucial to understand the role of programming languages in shaping this domain. The choice of a programming language can significantly impact the ease of development, performance, and scalability of AI and ML projects. This section will explore some of the most popular programming languages for AI and ML, highlighting their strengths and weaknesses to help you make an informed decision.

Python

Python has emerged as the undisputed leader in the AI and ML landscape thanks to its simplicity, readability, and extensive library support. Its syntax is clear and concise, allowing developers to focus on the logic and algorithms rather than getting bogged down by complex code structures. Python's vast ecosystem of libraries, such as Tensor-Flow, PyTorch, and scikit-learn, makes it an ideal choice for implementing various AI and ML techniques, including deep learning, natural language processing, and computer vision.

R

R is a powerful statistical programming language that has gained immense popularity among data scientists and statisticians. Its comprehensive statistical and graphical tools suite makes it an excellent choice for data analysis, visualization, and modeling. R's rich library support, including packages like caret, randomForest, and xgboost, enables developers to implement a wide range of ML algorithms easily. However, R's steep learning curve and less intuitive syntax may challenge beginners.

Java

Java, a versatile and widely used programming language, has also found its place in the AI and ML domain. Its platform independence, robustness, and strong object-oriented programming (OOP) capabilities make it suitable for large-scale, complex AI and ML projects. Java's extensive library support, such as Deeplearning4j, Weka, and Java-ML, facilitates the implementation of various ML algorithms and techniques. However, Java's verbosity and slower execution speed compared to Python may be a drawback for some developers.

C++

C++ is a high-performance programming language that offers fine-grained control over system resources, making it an attractive choice for computationally intensive AI and ML tasks. Its powerful OOP features and support for parallelism enable developers to build efficient and scalable AI and ML applications. Libraries like Shark, mlpack, and Dlib provide a solid foundation for implementing ML algorithms in C++. However, C++ has a steeper learning curve and lacks the extensive library support available in Python and R.

Julia

Julia is a relatively new programming language gaining traction in the AI and ML community. It combines the ease of use and readability of Python with the performance of C++, making it an appealing choice for developers. Julia's growing ecosystem of libraries, such as Flux, MLJ, and Knet, supports various AI and ML techniques. While Julia shows great promise, its relatively smaller community and limited library support compared to more established languages may concern some developers.

In conclusion, choosing a programming language for AI and ML projects largely depends on your specific requirements, existing skillset, and personal preferences. Python and R are excellent for their extensive library support and ease of use, while Java and C++ offer robustness and scalability for large-scale projects. With its blend of simplicity and performance, Julia is an exciting newcomer to the field. Ultimately, the key is to choose a language that enables you to effectively and efficiently bring your AI and ML ideas to life.

Machine Learning Libraries and Frameworks

In artificial intelligence (AI) and machine learning (ML), the right tools can make all the difference in the success of your projects. Machine learning libraries and frameworks are essential components that provide developers with pre-built algorithms, functions, and methods to simplify the process of creating and implementing ML models. This section will explore some of the most popular machine learning libraries and frameworks, discussing their features, advantages, and use cases.

Scikit-learn

Scikit-learn is an open-source Python library offering various machine learning algorithms for various tasks, including classification, regression, clustering, and dimensionality reduction. It is built on top of NumPy, SciPy, and Matplotlib, essential libraries for scientific computing in Python. Scikit-learn is known for its user-friendly interface, comprehensive documentation, and active community support. It is an excellent choice for beginners and experienced developers looking to implement traditional machine-learning techniques in their projects.

TensorFlow

Developed by Google, TensorFlow is an open-source machine learning framework that has gained immense popularity for its flexibility, scalability, and ability to work with deep learning models. TensorFlow supports multiple programming languages, including Python, C++, and Java, and can be used for various tasks such as image and speech recognition, natural language processing, and reinforcement learning. Its extensive ecosystem, including tools like TensorBoard for visualization and TensorFlow Extended (TFX) for production pipelines, makes it a powerful choice for research and production environments.

Keras

Keras is a high-level neural networks API written in Python and capable of running on top of TensorFlow, Microsoft Cognitive Toolkit, or Theano. It was designed to enable fast experimentation with deep neural networks and focuses on being user-friendly, modular, and extensible. Keras provides a simple interface for building and training complex neural network models, making it an excellent choice for developers new to deep learning or those who prefer a more intuitive approach to model creation.

PyTorch

Created by Facebook's AI Research lab, PyTorch is an open-source machine learning framework that has gained popularity for its dynamic computation graph, ease of debugging, and strong support for GPU acceleration. PyTorch is particularly well-suited for deep learning applications, offering a wide range of pre-built models and tools for computer vision, natural language processing, and reinforcement learning. Its "eager execution" mode allows developers to see the results of their code as they write it, making it easier to identify and fix errors in the development process.

XGBoost

XGBoost, short for eXtreme Gradient Boosting, is an open-source library that provides an efficient and scalable implementation of gradient-boosted decision trees. It is designed for speed and performance, with features like parallelization, regularization, and early stopping to prevent overfitting. XGBoost has been widely adopted in machine learning competitions and real-world applications due to its ability to handle large datasets and deliver accurate results. It supports multiple programming languages, including Python, R, Java, and Scala.

In conclusion, the choice of machine learning libraries and frameworks depends on your specific project requirements, programming language preferences, and level of expertise. By familiarizing yourself with these popular tools, you can make informed decisions and select the best options for your AI and ML projects. As you continue to explore the world of AI and ML development, remember that the right tools can significantly enhance your productivity and the quality of your work.

Data Visualization and Analysis Tools

In artificial intelligence (AI) and machine learning (ML), data visualization and analysis tools play a crucial role in understanding and interpreting the vast amounts of data generated by these technologies. These tools enable developers and data scientists to gain insights, identify patterns, and make informed decisions based on the data. This section will explore some of the most popular and widely used data visualization and analysis tools that can significantly enhance your AI and ML projects.

Matplotlib

Matplotlib is a versatile and powerful Python library for creating static, animated, and interactive visualizations. It offers many plotting options, including line plots, scatter plots, bar plots, and more. With its extensive customization options, Matplotlib allows users to create visually appealing and informative graphics that can effectively communicate the results of their AI and ML models.

Seaborn

Seaborn is another Python library built on top of Matplotlib, designed to simplify creating complex and aesthetically pleasing data visualizations. It has several built-in themes and color palettes to make it easy for users to create visually appealing plots. Seaborn also integrates seamlessly with the Pandas library, allowing for efficient data manipulation and analysis.

Plotly

Plotly is a popular open-source library for creating interactive and web-based visualizations in Python, R, and Julia. It offers various chart types, including scatter plots, line charts, bar charts, and more. Plotly's interactive features, such as tooltips, zooming, and panning, make it an excellent choice for presenting and exploring complex datasets in AI and ML projects.

Tableau

Tableau is a powerful data visualization and analysis tool that allows users to create interactive and shareable dashboards. With its intuitive drag-and-drop interface, Tableau enables users to quickly analyze large datasets and create visually appealing visualizations without programming knowledge. Tableau's integration with various data sources, such as databases, spreadsheets, and cloud services, makes it a popular choice for data-driven decision-making in AI and ML projects.

Jupyter Notebook

Jupyter Notebook is an open-source web application that allows users to create and share documents containing live code, equations, visualizations, and narrative text. It is widely used in the AI and ML community for data cleaning, transformation, and visualization, as well as for building and training models. Jupyter Notebook's interactive nature makes it an ideal tool for exploring data, testing hypotheses, and iterating on models.

In conclusion, selecting the right data visualization and analysis tools for your AI and ML projects is essential for effectively communicating your findings and making data-driven decisions. By familiarizing yourself with the various tools available, you can choose the ones that best suit your needs and enhance the overall success of your projects.

Choosing the Right Tools for Your AI and ML Projects

As we have traversed the landscape of artificial intelligence (AI) and machine learning (ML) development, we have encountered many tools and libraries that cater to the diverse needs of coders. The options are vast and varied, from programming languages to machine learning frameworks, deep learning libraries, and data visualization tools. In this concluding section, we provide guidance on selecting the most suitable tools for your AI and ML projects, ensuring you can harness these cutting-edge technologies' full potential.

The first step in choosing the right tools for your AI and ML projects is identifying your specific goals and requirements. Are you looking to develop a simple machine-learning model or delve into the complexities of deep learning? Are you working on a project requiring real-time data analysis or focusing on data visualization? By clearly defining your objectives, you can narrow down the tools and libraries that best serve your needs.

Next, consider your level of expertise and familiarity with programming languages. While Python is widely regarded as the go-to language for AI and ML development, other languages such as R, Java, and C++ offer robust libraries and frameworks. If you are already proficient in a particular language, it may be more efficient to leverage its capabilities rather than learn a new one from scratch. However, if you are starting your AI and ML journey, Python's user-friendly syntax and extensive resources make it an excellent choice.

The choice of machine learning libraries and frameworks largely depends on the type of model you wish to create and the level of customization you require. Scikit-learn is a popular choice for beginners due to its simplicity and ease of use, while TensorFlow and PyTorch offer more advanced features and flexibility for experienced developers. Be sure to explore the documentation and community support for each library, as these resources can significantly impact your learning curve and overall experience.

Deep learning libraries and tools like Keras, TensorFlow, and PyTorch cater to different preferences and use cases. Keras is known for its user-friendly interface and is ideal for those new to deep learning. TensorFlow and PyTorch provide more control over the underlying architecture and are preferred by researchers and professionals. Again, consider your project requirements and personal preferences when making your selection.

Data visualization and analysis tools are crucial for understanding and interpreting the results of your AI and ML models. Libraries such as Matplotlib, Seaborn, and Plotly offer a range of visualization options to suit various data types and presentation styles. Tools like Pandas and NumPy also facilitate data manipulation and analysis, streamlining the development process.

In conclusion, the choice of tools and libraries for your AI and ML projects is a critical decision that can significantly impact the success of your endeavors. By carefully considering your project goals, programming language preferences, and desired level of customization, you can confidently select the tools that will propel you toward achieving your AI and ML aspirations. Remember, mastering AI and ML is an ongoing process, and as you grow and evolve as a developer, so will your toolkit.

Chapter Summary

- AI and ML development involves a diverse range of languages, libraries, and tools that cater to different needs and preferences, making it essential for developers to explore these options and choose the right ones for their projects.
- Popular programming languages for AI and ML include Python, R, Java, C++, and Julia, each with strengths and weaknesses. Python and R are known for their extensive library support and ease of use, while Java and C++ offer robustness and scalability for large-scale projects.
- Machine learning libraries and frameworks like Scikit-learn, TensorFlow, Keras, PyTorch, and XGBoost provide developers with pre-built algorithms, functions, and methods to simplify creating and implementing ML models.
- Deep learning libraries and tools, including TensorFlow, Keras, PyTorch, Caffe, and Theano, enable developers to harness the full potential of deep learning techniques, such as neural networks, for various AI and ML applications.

- Data visualization and analysis tools, like Matplotlib, Seaborn, Plotly, Tableau, and Jupyter Notebook, play a crucial role in understanding and interpreting the vast amounts of data generated by AI and ML technologies.
- Identifying specific goals and requirements is the first step in choosing the right tools for AI and ML projects, followed by considering the level of expertise and familiarity with programming languages.
- The choice of machine learning libraries and frameworks largely depends on the type of model to be created and the level of customization required, while deep learning libraries cater to different preferences and use cases.
- Selecting the right tools and libraries for AI and ML projects is a critical decision that can significantly impact the success of the endeavors, and as developers grow and evolve, so will their toolkit.

4

DATA PREPARATION AND PREPROCESSING TECHNIQUES FOR MACHINE LEARNING

I n the constantly changing world of artificial intelligence (AI) and machine learning (ML), the role of data has become increasingly significant. As coders and developers, we must recognize that our ML models' success relies heavily on the quality and structure of the data we feed them. This chapter delves into the essential aspects of data preparation and preprocessing techniques, which are the foundation for building accurate and efficient ML models.

Data preparation and preprocessing encompass a wide range of techniques that aim to transform raw data into a format easily understood and utilized by ML algorithms. These techniques ensure that our models can extract meaningful insights and make accurate predictions. By investing time and effort into preparing and preprocessing our data, we can significantly enhance the performance of our ML models and, ultimately, the success of our AI applications.

In this chapter, we will explore the importance of data quality in machine learning and discuss various techniques to clean and handle missing values in our datasets. We will also delve into the art of feature engineering and selection, which can significantly impact the performance of our models. Furthermore, we will examine data transformation and scaling techniques that can help standardize and normalize our data for optimal model training.

By the end of this chapter, you will have a comprehensive understanding of the various data preparation and preprocessing techniques essential for successful machine learning projects. With this knowledge, you will be well-equipped to tackle the challenges of working with real-world data and building high-performing ML models. So, let's embark on this exciting journey and uncover the secrets to effective data preparation and preprocessing in AI and ML.

Understanding the Importance of Data Quality in Machine Learning

In the realm of artificial intelligence (AI) and machine learning (ML), the adage "garbage in, garbage out" rings truer than ever. As coders and developers, we must recognize the critical role that data quality plays in the success of our machine-learning models. In this section, we will delve into the significance of data quality, its impact on model performance, and the potential consequences of neglecting this crucial aspect of machine learning.

To begin with, let us consider the foundation of any machine learning project: the data. High-quality data is the lifeblood of machine learning algorithms, enabling them to learn patterns, make predictions, and, ultimately, solve complex problems. Even the most sophisticated algorithms will struggle to produce meaningful results without accurate, reliable, and relevant data. The quality of the data we feed into our models directly influences their ability to make accurate predictions and generate valuable insights.

We must consider several key dimensions of data quality when preparing our datasets for machine learning. These include:

- **Accuracy:** The degree to which the data reflects the true state of the world or the phenomenon being studied. Inaccurate data can lead to incorrect predictions and misguided decision-making.
- **Completeness:** The extent to which all necessary data points are present in the dataset. Missing or incomplete data can hinder the ability of machine learning algorithms to identify patterns and make accurate predictions.
- **Consistency:** The uniformity of data across different sources and formats. Inconsistent data can create confusion and ambiguity, making it difficult for algorithms to learn and generalize effectively.
- **Relevance:** The pertinence of the data to the problem at hand. Irrelevant data can introduce noise and distractions, impeding the ability of machine learning models to focus on the most essential features and relationships.
- **Timeliness:** The currency and freshness of the data. Outdated or stale data can lead to ill-equipped models to handle current or future scenarios.

Neglecting data quality can have far-reaching consequences for machine learning projects. Poor-quality data can result in less accurate, unreliable, and generalizable models for new situations. This, in turn, can lead to misguided decision-making, wasted resources, and, ultimately, a loss of trust in the power of AI and ML.

In conclusion, understanding the importance of data quality in machine learning is paramount for coders and developers who wish to harness the full potential of AI and ML technologies. By ensuring that our datasets are accurate, complete, consistent, relevant, and timely, we can lay the groundwork for machine learning models capable of delivering powerful insights and driving meaningful change. In the following sections, we will explore various data preparation and preprocessing techniques to help us achieve this goal and set our machine learning projects up for success.

Data Cleaning and Handling Missing Values

The adage "garbage in, garbage out" holds true in machine learning. The data quality fed into a model directly impacts its performance and accuracy. Data cleaning, therefore, is a crucial step in the machine learning pipeline. This section will delve into the importance of data cleaning and explore various techniques for handling missing values in your dataset.

The Importance of Data Cleaning

Data cleaning is identifying and correcting errors, inconsistencies, and inaccuracies in datasets. Raw data collected from various sources often contains noise, missing values, and outliers that can negatively affect the performance of machine learning algorithms. Cleaning the data ensures your model is trained on accurate and reliable information, leading to better predictions and insights.

Identifying Missing Values

Before handling missing values, it is essential to identify them in your dataset. Missing values can occur for various reasons, such as data entry errors, equipment malfunctions, or respondents not providing information in surveys. In most programming languages and libraries, missing values are represented as "NaN" (Not a Number) or "null."

Techniques for Handling Missing Values

There are several techniques for handling missing values in a dataset, each with advantages and disadvantages. The choice of technique depends on the nature of the data, the percentage of missing values, and the specific requirements of the machine learning model. Some common techniques include:

- **Deletion:** This method removes rows or columns with missing values from the dataset. While it is the most straightforward approach, deletion can lead to the loss of valuable information, especially if a significant portion of the data is missing.
- **Imputation:** Imputation involves replacing missing values with estimated values based on other available data. There are various imputation techniques, such as mean, median, or mode imputation for numerical data and the most frequent category imputation for categorical data. More advanced techniques include regression imputation and k-nearest neighbors imputation.
- **Interpolation:** This technique is used for time-series data, where missing values are estimated based on the values of neighboring data points. Linear interpolation is the most common method, but more advanced techniques like polynomial or spline interpolation can also be used.

Using algorithms that handle missing values: Some machine learning algorithms, such as decision trees and random forests, can handle missing values without the need for preprocessing. Depending on the specific implementation, these algorithms can either ignore the missing values or use them to make splits in the data.

Evaluating the Impact of Handling Missing Values

After applying a technique to handle missing values, evaluating its impact on the dataset and the machine learning model's performance is essential. This can be done by comparing the performance metrics of the model trained on the original dataset with the performance metrics of the model trained on the cleaned dataset. If the performance improves significantly, it indicates that the chosen technique effectively handles missing values.

In conclusion, data cleaning and handling missing values are critical steps in the machine learning pipeline. By ensuring that your dataset is free of errors and inconsistencies, you can significantly improve the performance and accuracy of your machine-learning models. Remember to carefully consider the nature of your data and your model's specific requirements when choosing a technique for handling missing values.

Feature Engineering and Selection for Optimal Model Performance

The adage "garbage in, garbage out" holds true in machine learning. The quality of the input data directly impacts the performance of the model. As such, feature engineering and selection are crucial in ensuring optimal model performance. In this section, we will delve into the art and science of feature engineering and selection, exploring the various techniques and strategies that can be employed to enhance the performance of machine learning models.

Feature engineering transforms raw data into meaningful and informative features that can be used as input for machine learning algorithms. This process often involves domain knowledge, creativity, and intuition to identify the most relevant features for a given problem. Some standard feature engineering techniques include:

- **Combining features:** This involves creating new features by combining two or more existing features. For example, in a dataset containing information about houses, one could create a new feature called "price per square foot" by dividing the price of the house by its square footage.

- **Binning:** This technique involves grouping continuous variables into discrete categories or bins. For instance, age can be binned into categories such as "young," "middle-aged," and "old."
- **Polynomial features:** This technique involves creating new features by raising existing features to power or combining them multiplicatively. For example, if a dataset contains features x and y, one could create new features x^2, y^2, and x*y.
- **One-hot encoding:** This technique converts categorical variables into binary features. For example, a feature representing the color of a car (red, blue, or green) can be converted into three binary features: "is_red," "is_blue," and "is_green."

On the other hand, feature selection identifies the most critical features from the original dataset or the engineered features. This is crucial because irrelevant or redundant features can negatively impact the model's performance. Some common feature selection techniques include:

- **Filter methods:** These techniques involve ranking features based on a specific metric, such as correlation with the target variable or mutual information, and selecting the top-ranked features.
- **Wrapper methods:** These techniques involve evaluating the performance of a machine learning model with different subsets of features and selecting the subset that yields the best performance. Examples of wrapper methods include forward selection, backward elimination, and recursive feature elimination.
- **Embedded methods:** These techniques involve selecting features as part of the model training process. For example, regularization techniques such as Lasso and Ridge

regression can penalize the inclusion of irrelevant features, effectively performing feature selection.

In conclusion, feature engineering and selection are essential steps in the data preparation process for machine learning. By carefully crafting informative features and selecting the most relevant ones, data scientists can significantly improve the performance of their models, leading to more accurate predictions and better decision-making.

The Impact of Effective Data Preparation on Machine Learning Success

In conclusion, the significance of data preparation and preprocessing techniques in artificial intelligence and machine learning cannot be overstated. As we have explored throughout this chapter, the quality of data fed into machine learning models is a critical determinant of their success. By ensuring that the data is clean, well-structured, and appropriately transformed, coders can unlock the true potential of AI and ML algorithms, leading to more accurate and reliable predictions.

The process of data cleaning and handling missing values is essential to maintain the integrity of the dataset. By identifying and addressing inconsistencies, outliers, and inaccuracies, coders can create a solid foundation for their machine-learning models. This step not only improves the algorithms' performance but also helps build trust in the results generated by the models.

Feature engineering and selection play a crucial role in optimizing model performance. By carefully crafting and selecting the most relevant features, coders can ensure that their models can capture the underlying patterns and relationships within the data. This, in turn, leads to more efficient and effective machine learning models that can deliver actionable insights and drive decision-making.

Data transformation and scaling techniques are vital in ensuring that the data is compatible with the requirements of machine learning algorithms. By applying appropriate transformations and scaling methods, coders can ensure that their models can process the data effectively and generate meaningful results. This step is particularly important when dealing with large and complex datasets, as it can significantly impact the speed and accuracy of the machine-learning process.

In summary, effective data preparation and preprocessing techniques are the backbone of successful machine-learning projects. By investing time and effort in these crucial steps, coders can significantly enhance the performance of their AI and ML models, leading to more accurate predictions and valuable insights. As the field of artificial intelligence and machine learning continues to evolve, the importance of data preparation and preprocessing will only grow, making it an essential skill for coders to master.

Chapter Summary

- Data preparation and preprocessing are crucial for building accurate and efficient machine learning (ML) models, as they ensure the quality and structure of the input data.
- Data quality is paramount in ML, directly influencing the model's ability to make accurate predictions and generate valuable insights. Key dimensions of data quality include accuracy, completeness, consistency, relevance, and timeliness.
- Data cleaning and handling missing values are essential steps in the ML pipeline, as they help maintain the integrity of the dataset and improve model performance.
- Feature engineering and selection are critical in optimizing model performance by creating meaningful features and selecting the most relevant ones for the given problem.
- Data transformation and scaling techniques ensure compatibility with ML algorithms, as they standardize and normalize the data for optimal model training.

- Common data transformation techniques include combining features, binning, polynomial features, one-hot encoding, and Box-Cox transformation.
- Common scaling techniques include Min-Max Scaling, Standardization (Z-score normalization), and Log Transformation.
- Effective data preparation and preprocessing techniques lay the foundation for successful ML projects, leading to more accurate predictions, valuable insights, and better decision-making.

5

SUPERVISED LEARNING ALGORITHMS: REGRESSION, CLASSIFICATION, AND DECISION TREES

I n the perpetually transforming world of artificial intelligence (AI) and machine learning (ML), supervised learning algorithms have emerged as a powerful tool for coders seeking to develop intelligent systems capable of making predictions and decisions based on data. As the name suggests, supervised learning involves training a model using labeled data where the correct output is known. This chapter delves into the fascinating realm of supervised learning algorithms, focusing on regression, classification, and decision trees and exploring their practical applications in real-world scenarios.

Supervised learning algorithms can be broadly categorized into two types: regression and classification. Regression algorithms are used to predict continuous values, such as the price of a house or the number of sales in a month. On the other hand, classification algorithms are employed to predict categorical values, such as whether an email is spam or if a customer will make a purchase. Decision trees, a versatile and popular technique, can be used for both regression and classification tasks, making them an essential topic of discussion in this chapter.

The supervised learning process begins with collecting a dataset containing input-output pairs, where the output is the desired outcome or target variable. The dataset is then divided into two parts: the training set and the testing set. The training set is used to build the model, while the testing set is reserved for evaluating the model's performance. The algorithm learns from the training data by adjusting its parameters to minimize errors between its predictions and output. Once the model is trained, it can predict new, unseen data.

Throughout this chapter, we will explore various regression techniques, such as linear regression and polynomial regression, and delve into classification algorithms, including logistic regression, k-nearest neighbors, and support vector machines. We will also unravel the power of decision trees and their ensemble counterparts, such as random forests and gradient-boosting machines. Each section will provide a comprehensive understanding of these algorithms' underlying concepts, mathematical foundations, and practical implementation.

Moreover, we will discuss real-world examples and applications of supervised learning algorithms, showcasing their potential in diverse fields such as finance, healthcare, marketing, and more. By the end of this chapter, you will have a solid grasp of the fundamentals of supervised learning algorithms and be equipped with the knowledge to harness their potential in your coding projects.

In conclusion, supervised learning algorithms offer a robust and versatile approach to solving a wide range of problems in AI and ML. By understanding the principles of regression, classification, and decision trees, coders can unlock the full potential of these powerful techniques and create intelligent systems capable of making accurate predictions and informed decisions based on data. So, let's embark on this exciting journey and delve into the fascinating world of supervised learning algorithms.

Exploring Regression Techniques for Predictive Modeling

Regression techniques hold a special place in supervised learning algorithms as they enable coders to create predictive models that can forecast continuous values. This section will delve into the intricacies of regression techniques, providing a comprehensive understanding of their applications and importance in machine learning.

The Essence of Regression Techniques

At the core of regression techniques is establishing relationships between variables. In the context of machine learning, these variables are often referred to as features or predictors (independent variables) and targets or responses (dependent variables). The primary objective of regression techniques is to create a model that can accurately predict the target variable based on the values of the predictor variables.

Linear Regression: The Foundation

Linear regression is the most fundamental and widely used regression technique in machine learning. It assumes a linear relationship between the predictor and target variables, which can be represented by a straight line. Linear regression aims to find the best-fitting line that minimizes the sum of the squared differences between the actual and predicted target values. This line is represented by the equation:

$$y = \beta_0 + \beta_1 x_1 + \beta_2 x_2 + \dots + \beta_n x_n + \varepsilon$$

Here, y is the target variable, x1, x2, ..., xn are the predictor variables, β0 is the intercept, β1, β2, ..., βn are the coefficients, and ε is the error term.

Expanding Horizons: Non-Linear Regression Techniques

While linear regression is a powerful tool, it may not always be suitable for modeling complex relationships between variables. This is where non-linear regression techniques come into play, allowing coders to model curved relationships between predictor and target variables. Some popular non-linear regression techniques include polynomial regression, exponential regression, and logistic regression.

Regularization Techniques: Tackling Overfitting

In machine learning, overfitting occurs when a model becomes too complex and captures the noise in the data, leading to poor generalization of new, unseen data. Regularization techniques, such as Ridge Regression, Lasso Regression, and Elastic Net, help mitigate overfitting by adding a penalty term to the regression equation. This penalty term discourages the model from assigning large weights to the predictor variables, thus preventing overfitting and improving the model's performance on new data.

Evaluating Regression Models: Performance Metrics

To assess the performance of regression models, coders can use various metrics, such as Mean Absolute Error (MAE), Mean Squared Error (MSE), Root Mean Squared Error (RMSE), and R-squared. These metrics provide valuable insights into the accuracy and reliability of the model, enabling coders to fine-tune their models and select the most appropriate regression technique for their specific problem.

In conclusion, regression techniques are indispensable tools for coders working with supervised learning algorithms. By understanding the nuances of linear and non-linear regression techniques, regularization methods, and performance metrics, coders can harness the power of predictive modeling to tackle a wide array of real-world problems.

Delving into Classification Algorithms for Categorical Data

As we venture deeper into supervised learning algorithms, it is essential to understand the significance of classification algorithms in handling categorical data. This section will explore the various classification techniques, their underlying principles, and how coders can effectively employ them to create powerful machine-learning models.

Classification algorithms are a subset of supervised learning techniques that focus on predicting categorical outcomes. In other words, these algorithms are designed to classify data points into distinct categories or classes based on their features. Some common examples of classification tasks include spam detection, medical diagnosis, and image recognition.

Let's now delve into some of the most widely used classification algorithms in machine learning.

- **Logistic Regression:** Despite its name, logistic regression is a classification algorithm that is particularly well-suited for binary classification problems, where the target variable has only two possible outcomes. It estimates the probability of an instance belonging to a specific class using the logistic function, which outputs a value between 0 and 1. The predicted class is then determined based on a threshold value, typically set at 0.5.
- **K-Nearest Neighbors (KNN):** KNN is a simple yet powerful classification algorithm that can be used for both binary and multi-class problems. It operates on the principle of proximity, where an instance is classified based on the majority class of its 'k' nearest neighbors. The value of 'k' is a user-defined parameter that determines the number of neighbors to consider when making predictions. KNN is particularly effective when dealing

with datasets that have well-defined boundaries between classes.

- **Support Vector Machines (SVM):** SVM is a versatile classification algorithm that handles linear and non-linearly separable data. It works by finding the optimal hyperplane that best separates the classes in the feature space. For non-linearly separable data, SVM employs the kernel trick to transform the data into a higher-dimensional space where a linear separation is possible. SVM is known for its robustness and ability to handle high-dimensional data.
- **Naïve Bayes:** This classification algorithm is based on the Bayes theorem and assumes that the features are conditionally independent given the class label. Despite its simplicity and the naïve assumption of feature independence, Naïve Bayes has proven effective in various real-world applications, particularly in text classification and sentiment analysis.
- **Decision Trees:** As discussed in the previous section, decision trees are a powerful classification algorithm that can handle both categorical and continuous data. They work by recursively splitting the data based on the feature that provides the highest information gain, resulting in a tree-like structure with decision nodes and leaf nodes representing the class labels.

In conclusion, classification algorithms are crucial in machine learning, enabling coders to tackle various categorical data problems. By understanding each algorithm's underlying principles and strengths, you can make informed decisions when selecting the most appropriate technique for your specific use case. In the next section, we will unravel the power of decision trees in machine learning and explore their numerous applications.

Unraveling the Power of Decision Trees in Machine Learning

Decision trees hold a special place in the fascinating world of machine learning due to their simplicity, interpretability, and versatility. As a coder, understanding the power of decision trees will enable you to easily harness their potential in solving complex problems. In this section, we will delve into the inner workings of decision trees, their advantages, and how they can be applied in various machine learning tasks.

The Essence of Decision Trees

At their core, decision trees are flowchart-like structures that help in making decisions based on certain conditions. They consist of nodes representing the conditions or attributes and branches, which signify the possible outcomes of those conditions. The tree starts with a root node, which branches into subsequent nodes until a final decision is reached at the leaf nodes.

In the context of machine learning, decision trees are used for both regression and classification tasks. They work by recursively splitting the input data into subsets based on the most significant attribute, ultimately leading to a prediction. The elegance of decision trees lies in their ability to mimic human decision-making processes, making them easily interpretable and relatable.

Advantages of Decision Trees

Decision trees offer several benefits that make them a popular choice among coders and data scientists:

- **Interpretability:** Decision trees are easy to understand and visualize, even for those with limited knowledge of machine learning. This transparency allows stakeholders to trust and validate the model's predictions.

- **Minimal Data Preprocessing:** Unlike other algorithms, decision trees do not require extensive data preprocessing, such as normalization or scaling. They can handle missing values, outliers, and categorical data with ease.
- **Non-Parametric Nature:** Decision trees make no assumptions about the underlying data distribution, making them suitable for various applications.
- **Fast Training and Prediction:** Decision trees can be trained quickly and provide predictions in logarithmic time, making them efficient for large datasets.

Practical Applications of Decision Trees

The versatility of decision trees allows them to be employed in various domains, including:

- **Healthcare:** Decision trees can predict the likelihood of a disease based on patient symptoms, aiding in early diagnosis and treatment.
- **Finance:** In the financial sector, decision trees can help assess credit risk, detect fraudulent transactions, and predict stock prices.
- **Marketing:** Decision trees can assist in customer segmentation, enabling targeted marketing campaigns and personalized recommendations.
- **Manufacturing:** In the manufacturing industry, decision trees can be used for quality control, identifying the root cause of defects, and optimizing production processes.

Unleashing the Power of Decision Trees

As a coder, mastering decision trees will equip you with a powerful tool in your machine-learning arsenal. By understanding their inner workings and leveraging their strengths, you can confidently tackle a wide array of problems. In the next section, we will explore practical applications and real-world examples of supervised learning, further solidifying your knowledge and skills in this exciting field.

Practical Applications and Real-World Examples of Supervised Learning

As we delve deeper into artificial intelligence (AI) and machine learning (ML), it is essential to understand the practical applications and real-world examples of supervised learning algorithms. These algorithms have been successfully employed in various industries, solving complex problems and enhancing decision-making processes. This section will explore some of the most notable applications of regression, classification, and decision trees in different domains.

- **Healthcare:** Supervised learning algorithms have revolutionized the healthcare industry by enabling the development of predictive models for disease diagnosis and treatment. For instance, regression techniques are used to predict patient outcomes based on their medical history and vital signs, while classification algorithms help identify diseases such as cancer, diabetes, and heart disorders. Decision trees, on the other hand, are employed to determine the most effective treatment plans for patients based on their unique medical conditions.
- **Finance:** In the financial sector, supervised learning algorithms play a crucial role in predicting stock prices, assessing credit risk, and detecting fraudulent transactions. Regression models are used to forecast future stock prices based on historical data, while classification algorithms help banks and financial institutions determine the creditworthiness of borrowers. Decision trees identify potential fraud patterns and flag suspicious transactions for further investigation.
- **Marketing:** The marketing domain has also benefited from the power of supervised learning algorithms. Regression

techniques predict customer lifetime value, allowing businesses to allocate resources more effectively and target high-value customers. Classification algorithms help in customer segmentation and the identification of potential target markets. Decision trees optimize marketing campaigns by identifying the most effective channels and strategies for reaching specific customer segments.

- **Manufacturing:** In the manufacturing industry, supervised learning algorithms are used to optimize production processes, reduce waste, and improve product quality. Regression models help predict equipment failure and maintenance requirements, while classification algorithms are employed to detect defects in products during the quality control process. Decision trees optimize production schedules and resource allocation, ensuring manufacturing operations run smoothly and efficiently.
- **Transportation:** Supervised learning algorithms have also significantly contributed to the transportation sector. Regression techniques predict travel times and optimize route planning, while classification algorithms help identify traffic patterns and congestion hotspots. Decision trees are employed to improve traffic signal timings and enhance the overall efficiency of transportation systems.

In conclusion, supervised learning algorithms have proven invaluable tools for coders in various industries, enabling them to develop predictive models and make data-driven decisions. By harnessing the potential of regression, classification, and decision trees, coders can create innovative solutions to complex problems and contribute to advancing AI and ML technologies. As we continue to explore the capabilities of these algorithms, we can expect to see even more groundbreaking applications and real-world examples in the future.

Harnessing the Potential of Supervised Learning Algorithms for Coders

In this final section of our exploration into supervised learning algorithms, we shall reflect on these techniques' immense potential for coders and the broader world of artificial intelligence and machine learning. By understanding and mastering regression, classification, and decision trees, coders can unlock a treasure trove of opportunities to create innovative solutions and contribute to the ever-evolving field of AI and ML.

Throughout this chapter, we have delved into the intricacies of supervised learning algorithms, beginning with an introduction to the fundamental concepts and techniques. We then explored the world of regression techniques, which enable coders to create predictive models for continuous data. By understanding linear and logistic regression, coders can harness the power of these algorithms to make accurate predictions and inform decision-making processes.

As we ventured further into supervised learning, we examined classification algorithms essential for handling categorical data. Techniques such as k-Nearest Neighbors, Support Vector Machines, and Naïve Bayes allow coders to classify data points into distinct categories, creating models that can predict outcomes and identify patterns in complex datasets.

Our journey then led us to the fascinating world of decision trees, a powerful and versatile tool in the machine learning toolbox. By understanding the principles of entropy, information gain, and tree pruning, coders can create robust and interpretable models that can be applied to a wide range of real-world problems.

This chapter also highlighted practical applications and real-world examples of supervised learning algorithms, demonstrating their immense potential in various industries and sectors. From healthcare and finance to marketing and transportation, these techniques are revolutionizing how we approach problem-solving and decision-making.

As we conclude our exploration into supervised learning algorithms, coders need to recognize the importance of continuous learning and adaptation in the ever-evolving world of AI and ML. By staying abreast of the latest developments and refining their skills, coders can harness the full potential of these powerful techniques and contribute to advancing this exciting field.

In summary, the world of supervised learning algorithms offers a wealth of opportunities for coders eager to make their mark in AI and ML. By mastering regression, classification, and decision trees, coders can create innovative solutions that have the potential to transform industries and improve the lives of people around the world. The future of AI and ML is bright, and with the power of supervised learning algorithms at their fingertips, coders are poised to play a pivotal role in shaping this exciting frontier.

Chapter Summary

- Supervised learning algorithms are powerful tools in AI and ML, enabling coders to develop intelligent systems capable of making predictions and decisions based on data. They can be broadly categorized into regression and classification techniques, with decision trees being versatile enough for both tasks.
- Regression techniques focus on predicting continuous values and involve establishing relationships between variables. Linear regression is the most fundamental technique, while non-linear regression techniques, such as polynomial regression, can model more complex relationships.
- Classification algorithms are designed to classify data points into distinct categories based on their features. Some widely used classification techniques include logistic regression, k-nearest neighbors, support vector machines, and naïve Bayes.

- Decision trees are flowchart-like structures that help make decisions based on certain conditions. They are simple, interpretable, and versatile, making them popular in machine learning for both regression and classification tasks.
- Supervised learning algorithms have practical applications in various industries, such as healthcare, finance, marketing, manufacturing, and transportation. They help in solving complex problems and enhancing decision-making processes.
- Performance metrics, such as Mean Absolute Error (MAE), Mean Squared Error (MSE), Root Mean Squared Error (RMSE), and R-squared, are essential for evaluating the performance of regression models and fine-tuning them for optimal results.
- Regularization techniques, such as Ridge Regression, Lasso Regression, and Elastic Net, help mitigate overfitting in regression models by adding a penalty term to the regression equation, preventing overfitting and improving the model's performance on new data.
- Continuous learning and adaptation are crucial for coders in the ever-evolving world of AI and ML. By mastering regression, classification, and decision trees, coders can create innovative solutions that have the potential to transform industries and improve the lives of people around the world.

6

UNSUPERVISED LEARNING ALGORITHMS: CLUSTERING, DIMENSIONALITY REDUCTION, AND ASSOCIATION RULES

I n the continuously evolving landscape of artificial intelligence (AI) and machine learning (ML), unsupervised learning algorithms have emerged as a powerful tool for coders seeking to uncover hidden patterns and structures within complex datasets. Unlike supervised learning, where algorithms are trained on labeled data to make predictions, unsupervised learning algorithms work with unlabeled data, allowing them to identify patterns and relationships that may not be immediately apparent. This chapter delves into the fascinating realm of unsupervised learning, exploring its various techniques, applications, and real-world examples.

Unsupervised learning algorithms can be broadly categorized into three main types: **clustering, dimensionality reduction**, and **association rules.** Each technique serves a unique purpose in data analysis, offering valuable insights that can be harnessed to drive decision-making and optimize processes.

Clustering techniques, such as K-Means, Hierarchical, and DBSCAN, are used to group similar data points together based on their features. This can be particularly useful in tasks like customer segmentation, anomaly detection, and image segmentation, where understanding the underlying structure of the data is crucial.

Dimensionality reduction methods, including Principal Component Analysis (PCA), t-Distributed Stochastic Neighbor Embedding (t-SNE), and Uniform Manifold Approximation and Projection (UMAP), are designed to reduce the number of features in a dataset while preserving its essential characteristics. By simplifying high-dimensional data, these techniques can improve the performance of other machine-learning algorithms and facilitate data visualization.

Association rules, such as the Apriori and Eclat algorithms, are employed to discover relationships between variables in large datasets. These rules can identify frequent item sets and generate insights into the associations between different items, which can be invaluable in fields like market basket analysis and recommender systems.

This chapter will delve deeper into these unsupervised learning techniques, providing a comprehensive understanding of their inner workings, strengths, and limitations. We will also explore practical applications and real-world examples, demonstrating the immense potential of unsupervised learning algorithms in various industries and domains.

In conclusion, unsupervised learning algorithms offer a powerful means of extracting valuable insights from complex, unlabeled data. By mastering these techniques, coders can unlock the full potential of AI and ML, harnessing the power of unsupervised learning to drive innovation and create a better future.

Clustering Techniques: K-Means, Hierarchical, and DBSCAN

In unsupervised learning algorithms, clustering techniques hold a prominent position. These methods aim to identify and group similar data points based on their features, thereby unveiling hidden patterns and structures within the data. This section will delve into three popular clustering techniques: K-Means, Hierarchical, and DBSCAN. By understanding their underlying principles and applications, coders can harness the power of these algorithms to tackle complex problems in AI and ML.

K-Means Clustering

K-Means is a widely-used clustering algorithm known for its simplicity and efficiency. The primary goal of this method is to partition the data into 'K' distinct clusters, where each data point belongs to the cluster with the nearest mean. The algorithm follows an iterative process, which includes:

1. **Initialization:** Randomly select 'K' data points as the initial cluster centroids.
2. **Assignment:** Assign each data point to the nearest centroid.
3. **Update:** Calculate the new centroid for each cluster by taking the mean of all the data points within that cluster.
4. **Repeat steps 2 and 3** until convergence is achieved, i.e., the centroids no longer change significantly.

Despite its popularity, K-Means has some limitations. The algorithm is sensitive to the initial placement of centroids and may converge to a local minimum. Additionally, it assumes that clusters are spherical and evenly sized, which may not always be the case in real-world data.

Hierarchical Clustering

Hierarchical clustering is another powerful technique that builds a tree-like structure to represent the relationships between data points. This method can be classified into two types: agglomerative (bottom-up) and divisive (top-down). In agglomerative clustering, each data point starts as an individual cluster, and the algorithm iteratively merges the closest clusters until only one cluster remains. Conversely, divisive clustering begins with a single cluster containing all data points and recursively splits it into smaller clusters.

The key to hierarchical clustering is the choice of distance metric and linkage criteria. Common distance metrics include Euclidean, Manhattan, and cosine distances, while linkage criteria can be single, complete, average, or Ward's method. The resulting hierarchical structure can be visualized using a dendrogram, which helps determine the optimal number of clusters.

DBSCAN (Density-Based Spatial Clustering of Applications with Noise)

DBSCAN is a density-based clustering algorithm that identifies clusters as dense regions of data points separated by areas of lower point density. Unlike K-Means and hierarchical clustering, DBSCAN does not require specifying the number of clusters beforehand. Instead, it relies on two parameters: a distance 'ε' and a minimum number of points 'MinPts'.

The algorithm defines a neighborhood around each data point within the distance 'ε'. If a data point has at least 'MinPts' neighbors, it is considered a core point and forms a cluster. Border points, which have fewer than 'MinPts' neighbors but are within the 'ε' distance of a core point, are also assigned to the cluster. All other points are considered noise.

DBSCAN is particularly useful for discovering clusters of arbitrary shapes and filtering out noise. However, it may struggle with clusters of varying densities and is sensitive to the choice of parameters.

In conclusion, clustering techniques such as K-Means, Hierarchical, and DBSCAN offer powerful tools for uncovering hidden structures within data. By understanding their principles and limitations, coders can effectively apply these algorithms to various AI and ML problems. As we explore unsupervised learning algorithms, we will delve into dimensionality reduction methods and association rules, further expanding our toolkit for tackling complex data-driven challenges.

Dimensionality Reduction Methods: PCA, t-SNE, and UMAP

In artificial intelligence and machine learning, data is the lifeblood that fuels the algorithms and models that drive innovation. However, as the volume and complexity of data increase, it becomes increasingly challenging to process and analyze it effectively. This is where dimensionality reduction methods come into play. In this section, we will delve into three popular techniques: Principal Component Analysis (PCA), t-Distributed Stochastic Neighbor Embedding (t-SNE), and Uniform Manifold Approximation and Projection (UMAP).

Principal Component Analysis (PCA)

PCA is a widely used linear dimensionality reduction technique that aims to identify the most significant variables in a dataset while preserving as much information as possible. It transforms the original data into a new set of orthogonal variables called principal components. These components are linear combinations of the original variables, ordered by the amount of variance they explain. The first principal component accounts for the largest possible variance, while each subsequent component explains the highest possible remaining variance under the constraint of being orthogonal to the preceding components.

In practical terms, PCA can reduce the computational cost and noise in the data, making it easier to visualize and analyze. It is particularly useful when dealing with high-dimensional datasets, such as image or gene expression data.

t-Distributed Stochastic Neighbor Embedding (t-SNE)

While PCA is a linear technique, t-SNE is a non-linear method designed to visualize high-dimensional data in a low-dimensional space, typically two or three dimensions. It minimizes the divergence between two probability distributions: one that measures pairwise similarities in the high-dimensional space and another that measures pairwise similarities in the low-dimensional space.

The main advantage of t-SNE over PCA is its ability to preserve local structures in the data, making it particularly suitable for visualizing complex datasets with non-linear relationships. However, t-SNE can be computationally expensive and sensitive to hyperparameters, which may require fine-tuning to achieve optimal results.

Uniform Manifold Approximation and Projection (UMAP)

UMAP is a relatively new dimensionality reduction technique that combines the strengths of both PCA and t-SNE. It is a non-linear method that aims to preserve both local and global structures in the data while being computationally efficient. UMAP works by constructing a high-dimensional graph representation of the data and optimizing a low-dimensional graph to be as structurally similar as possible.

One of the key advantages of UMAP is its scalability, making it suitable for large datasets. It is also less sensitive to hyperparameters than t-SNE, making it easier to use and interpret.

In conclusion, dimensionality reduction methods such as PCA, t-SNE, and UMAP are powerful tools that help coders and data scientists navigate the complexities of high-dimensional data. By understanding the strengths and limitations of each technique, practitioners can harness their potential to uncover hidden patterns, simplify data visualization, and, ultimately, enhance the performance of machine learning models.

Association Rules: Apriori and Eclat Algorithms

This section will delve into the fascinating world of association rules, a powerful unsupervised learning technique that can help us uncover hidden patterns and relationships within large datasets. We will focus on two widely used algorithms, Apriori and Eclat, and explore their inner workings, strengths, and limitations. By the end of this section, you will have a solid understanding of these algorithms and be well-equipped to apply them in your AI and ML projects.

Association rules are unsupervised learning algorithms that aim to discover interesting relationships between variables in large datasets. These relationships, often represented as "if-then" rules, can provide valuable insights into the underlying structure of the data and help us make better decisions. For example, an association rule in a retail dataset might reveal that customers who purchase diapers are also likely to buy baby wipes. This information can be used to optimize product placement, marketing strategies, and inventory management.

Apriori Algorithm

The Apriori algorithm, introduced by Rakesh Agrawal and Ramakrishnan Srikant in 1994, is a classic method for mining frequent item sets and generating association rules. The algorithm operates iteratively, starting with single-item sets and gradually expanding to larger itemsets while pruning the search space based on a user-defined minimum support threshold.

The key idea behind the Apriori algorithm is the Apriori principle, which states that if an itemset is frequent, then all its subsets must also be frequent. Conversely, if an itemset is infrequent, all its supersets must also be infrequent. This principle allows the algorithm to efficiently prune the search space and focus only on the most promising itemsets.

The Apriori algorithm consists of two main steps:

1. **Frequent Itemset Generation:** In this step, the algorithm iteratively generates candidate itemsets and computes their support (i.e., the proportion of transactions containing the itemset). Itemsets that meet the minimum support threshold are considered frequent and are used to generate larger candidate itemsets in the next iteration.

2. **Rule Generation:** Once all frequent item sets have been identified, the algorithm generates association rules by considering all possible combinations of items within each item set. Rules that meet the user-defined minimum confidence threshold (i.e., the conditional probability of the consequent given the antecedent) are considered valid and are returned as output.

Eclat Algorithm

The Eclat algorithm, proposed by Christian Borgelt in 1999, is another popular method for mining frequent item sets and generating association rules. Unlike the Apriori algorithm, which uses a horizontal data representation (i.e., transactions and their items), the Eclat algorithm employs a vertical data representation (i.e., items and their transactions).

The main advantage of the Eclat algorithm is its efficiency, as it avoids the repeated computation of itemset supports and leverages set intersection operations to identify frequent itemsets quickly. The algorithm operates in a depth-first search manner, recursively exploring the itemset lattice and pruning the search space based on the minimum support threshold.

In summary, association rules are a powerful unsupervised learning technique that can help us uncover hidden patterns and relationships within large datasets. The Apriori and Eclat algorithms are two widely used methods for mining frequent item sets and generating association rules, each with strengths and limitations. By understanding the inner workings of these algorithms and applying them to your projects, you can harness the power of unsupervised learning algorithms to gain valuable insights and make better decisions.

Practical Applications and Real-World Examples

Unsupervised learning algorithms have been making waves in artificial intelligence and machine learning, proving invaluable tools for coders and data scientists. These algorithms can uniquely identify patterns and relationships within data without the need for explicit guidance or labeled data. This section will explore some practical applications and real-world examples of unsupervised learning algorithms, showcasing their versatility and potential to revolutionize various industries.

Customer Segmentation in Marketing

Understanding customer behavior is crucial for developing targeted and effective campaigns in marketing. Clustering techniques, such as K-Means and Hierarchical clustering, can segment customers based on their purchasing habits, demographics, and preferences. This segmentation allows businesses to tailor their marketing strategies to specific customer groups, increasing customer satisfaction and loyalty.

Anomaly Detection in Finance

The finance industry is no stranger to the importance of identifying unusual patterns and activities. Unsupervised learning algorithms, particularly clustering methods like DBSCAN, can detect anomalies in financial data, such as fraudulent transactions or irregular trading activities. Financial institutions can swiftly mitigate potential risks and protect their clients' assets by identifying these outliers.

Recommender Systems in E-commerce

Online shopping platforms constantly seek ways to enhance the user experience and increase sales. Dimensionality reduction techniques, such as PCA and t-SNE, can be utilized to analyze customer browsing and purchasing data, enabling the development of personalized recommender systems. These systems provide users with tailored product suggestions based on their preferences and behavior, ultimately driving sales and customer satisfaction.

Natural Language Processing

The field of natural language processing (NLP) has dramatically benefited from unsupervised learning algorithms. Techniques like topic modeling, which employs dimensionality reduction methods like Latent Dirichlet Allocation (LDA), can analyze and categorize large volumes of text data. This can be particularly useful for sentiment analysis, document classification, and information retrieval.

Bioinformatics and Genomics

The rapidly growing field of bioinformatics and genomics has embraced unsupervised learning algorithms to make sense of the vast amounts of data generated by modern sequencing technologies. Clustering and dimensionality reduction techniques can be applied to identify patterns and relationships within genetic data, leading to new insights into gene function, disease mechanisms, and potential therapeutic targets.

In conclusion, unsupervised learning algorithms have demonstrated immense potential across various industries and applications. By harnessing the power of these algorithms, coders and data scientists can uncover hidden patterns and relationships within data, leading to innovative solutions and a deeper understanding of the world around us. As the field of artificial intelligence and machine learning continues to evolve, there is no doubt that unsupervised learning algorithms will play an increasingly prominent role in shaping our future.

Harnessing the Power of Unsupervised Learning Algorithms

As we reach the end of our exploration into the fascinating world of unsupervised learning algorithms, we must reflect on the immense potential these techniques hold for coders and data scientists alike. By delving into clustering, dimensionality reduction, and association rules, we have uncovered powerful tools that can transform how we analyze and interpret data, ultimately leading to more informed decision-making and innovative solutions.

This chapter has examined various clustering techniques, such as K-Means, Hierarchical, and DBSCAN, each with unique strengths and applications. These methods enable us to group data points based on their similarities, revealing hidden patterns and structures within the data. By harnessing the power of clustering algorithms, coders can develop more efficient and targeted solutions to complex problems, ranging from customer segmentation to image recognition.

Dimensionality reduction methods, including PCA, t-SNE, and UMAP, have further broadened our understanding of unsupervised learning algorithms. By reducing the number of variables in a dataset while preserving its essential features, these techniques allow us to visualize high-dimensional data more comprehensively. This not only aids in data exploration and interpretation but also helps improve the performance of other machine-learning models by reducing noise and computational complexity.

Lastly, we delved into association rules, focusing on the Apriori and Eclat algorithms. These techniques enable us to uncover relationships between items in a dataset, providing valuable insights into customer behavior, market trends, and more. By leveraging the power of association rules, coders can develop intelligent recommendation systems, optimize marketing strategies, and enhance the overall user experience.

Throughout this chapter, we have also highlighted practical applications and real-world examples, demonstrating the versatility and relevance of unsupervised learning algorithms in today's data-driven world. From healthcare and finance to retail and social media, these techniques are revolutionizing how we approach problem-solving and decision-making.

In conclusion, unsupervised learning algorithms offer a wealth of opportunities for coders and data scientists to unlock the hidden potential within their data. By mastering these techniques, you will be well-equipped to tackle complex challenges, drive innovation, and contribute to the ever-evolving field of artificial intelligence and machine learning. So, as you embark on your journey into unsupervised learning, remember to harness the power of these algorithms and let your creativity and curiosity guide you toward new discoveries and breakthroughs.

Chapter Summary

- Unsupervised learning algorithms work with unlabeled data, allowing them to identify patterns and relationships that may not be immediately apparent.
- Clustering techniques, such as K-Means, Hierarchical, and DBSCAN, group similar data points together based on their features, revealing hidden patterns and structures within the data.
- Dimensionality reduction methods, including PCA, t-SNE, and UMAP, reduce the number of features in a dataset while preserving its essential characteristics, simplifying high-dimensional data, and improving the performance of other machine learning algorithms.
- Association rules, such as the Apriori and Eclat algorithms, discover relationships between variables in large datasets, providing valuable insights into customer behavior, market trends, and more.
- Unsupervised learning algorithms have practical applications across various industries, including marketing, finance, e-commerce, natural language processing, and bioinformatics.

- Clustering techniques can be used for tasks like customer segmentation, anomaly detection, and image segmentation, while dimensionality reduction methods can facilitate data visualization and analysis.
- Association rules can be employed in market basket analysis and recommender systems, helping businesses optimize product placement, marketing strategies, and inventory management.
- Mastering unsupervised learning techniques can equip coders and data scientists to tackle complex challenges, drive innovation, and contribute to the ever-evolving field of artificial intelligence and machine learning.

7

DEEP LEARNING AND NEURAL NETWORKS: ARCHITECTURES, ACTIVATION FUNCTIONS, AND TRAINING TECHNIQUES

W ithin the ceaselessly advancing realm of technology, artificial intelligence (AI) and machine learning (ML) have emerged as powerful tools transforming how we live, work, and interact with the world around us. Deep learning is at the heart of this revolution, a subset of machine learning that has garnered significant attention and investment in recent years. This chapter delves into the fascinating realm of deep learning and neural networks, exploring their architectures, activation functions, and training techniques that enable coders to harness their full potential.

Deep learning is a machine learning technique that teaches computers to learn by example, much like humans. It involves using artificial neural networks, which are inspired by the structure and function of the human brain. These networks consist of interconnected layers of nodes or neurons that work together to process, analyze, and make sense of vast data. The ability of deep learning algorithms to automatically learn and improve from experience without being explicitly programmed has made them indispensable in various applications, ranging from natural language processing and computer vision to speech recognition and recommendation systems.

Neural networks are the backbone of deep learning, and their architectures play a crucial role in determining their performance and capabilities. This chapter will explore various neural network architectures, such as feedforward networks, recurrent networks, and convolutional networks, each with unique strengths and applications. Understanding these architectures will enable coders to select the most suitable one for their specific tasks and challenges.

Activation functions are another essential component of neural networks, as they determine the output of a neuron based on its input. These functions introduce non-linearity into the network, allowing it to learn complex patterns and relationships in the data. We will discuss different types of activation functions, such as sigmoid, ReLU, and softmax, and their applications in various contexts.

Training a neural network is a critical step in the deep learning process, as it involves adjusting the weights and biases of the network to minimize the error between the predicted and actual outputs. This chapter will cover various training techniques, such as gradient descent, backpropagation, and regularization, which are essential for achieving optimal performance in deep learning models.

Finally, we will examine real-world applications of AI and ML in coding, showcasing how deep learning and neural networks solve complex problems and create innovative solutions across various industries. This will provide a glimpse into the future of deep learning and neural networks, highlighting their potential to revolutionize the way we approach coding and problem-solving in the future.

Join us on this exciting journey as we unravel the mysteries of deep learning and neural networks, equipping you with the knowledge and skills to harness their power and transform the world of coding.

Exploring Various Neural Network Architectures

In artificial intelligence and machine learning, deep learning has emerged as a powerful tool for solving complex problems. At the heart of deep learning lies the concept of neural networks, which are inspired by the structure and function of the human brain. In this section, we will delve into the world of neural network architectures, exploring their various forms and understanding how they contribute to the development of intelligent systems.

Feedforward Neural Networks

The most basic and widely used neural network architecture is the feedforward neural network (FNN). In this type of network, information flows in one direction, from the input layer through one or more hidden layers and finally to the output layer. Each layer consists of interconnected nodes or neurons, which process the input data and pass it on to the next layer. FNNs are particularly useful for pattern recognition, classification, and regression tasks.

Convolutional Neural Networks

Convolutional neural networks (CNNs) are a specialized type of neural network designed to process grid-like data, such as images or speech signals. CNNs consist of multiple layers, including convolutional layers, pooling layers, and fully connected layers. The convolutional layers apply filters to the input data, extracting features such as edges, corners, and textures. Pooling layers reduce the spatial dimensions of the data, while fully connected layers combine the extracted features to make predictions. CNNs have achieved state-of-the-art results in image recognition, natural language processing, and speech recognition tasks.

Recurrent Neural Networks

Recurrent neural networks (RNNs) are designed to handle sequential data, such as time series or text. Unlike feedforward networks, RNNs have connections that loop back, allowing them to maintain a hidden state that can capture information from previous time steps. This architecture enables RNNs to learn patterns and dependencies in the input data over time. RNNs have been successfully applied to language modeling, machine translation, and speech recognition tasks. However, they can suffer from issues like vanishing or exploding gradients, hindering their ability to learn long-range dependencies.

Long Short-Term Memory Networks

To address the limitations of RNNs, long short-term memory (LSTM) networks were introduced. LSTMs are a type of RNN that incorporates a more sophisticated memory cell capable of learning long-range dependencies in the data. This is achieved through gating mechanisms, which control the flow of information into and out of the memory cell. LSTMs have been widely adopted in various applications, such as text generation, sentiment analysis, and video classification.

Generative Adversarial Networks

Generative adversarial networks (GANs) are a relatively recent addition to the neural network landscape. GANs consist of two neural networks, a generator and a discriminator, which are trained simultaneously in a competitive fashion. The generator learns to create realistic data samples, while the discriminator learns to distinguish between real and generated samples. This adversarial process generates high-quality data, making GANs particularly useful for tasks such as image synthesis, style transfer, and data augmentation.

In conclusion, the diverse range of neural network architectures available today enables researchers and practitioners to tackle many complex problems in artificial intelligence and machine learning. By understanding the strengths and limitations of each architecture, coders can make informed decisions about which approach is best suited for their specific application. As deep learning continues to evolve, we expect to see even more innovative and powerful neural network architectures emerge, further expanding the possibilities for AI and ML in coding.

Activation Functions: Types and Applications

In the fascinating world of deep learning and neural networks, activation functions play a crucial role in determining the output of a neuron. These functions introduce non-linearity into the network, allowing it to learn complex patterns and solve intricate problems. In this section, we will delve into the various types of activation functions, their applications, and how they contribute to the overall performance of a neural network.

Understanding Activation Functions

An activation function is a mathematical equation that determines the output of a neuron based on its input. It takes the weighted sum of the inputs and biases and then applies a specific function to produce the final output. The primary purpose of an activation function is to introduce non-linearity into the network, enabling it to learn and adapt to complex data patterns.

Types of Activation Functions

Several activation functions are used in deep learning, each with unique characteristics and applications. Some of the most commonly used activation functions include:

- **Sigmoid Function:** The sigmoid function is a smooth, S-shaped curve that maps input values to a range between 0 and 1. It is widely used in binary classification problems, as it can easily differentiate between two classes. However, it is susceptible to the vanishing gradient problem, which can slow down the learning process.
- **Hyperbolic Tangent (tanh) Function:** The tanh function is similar to the sigmoid function but maps input values to a range between -1 and 1. It is more suitable for problems where the output needs to be centered around zero. Like the sigmoid function, it also suffers from the vanishing gradient problem.
- **Rectified Linear Unit (ReLU) Function:** The ReLU function is a popular choice for deep learning, as it is computationally efficient and helps mitigate the vanishing gradient problem. It outputs the input value if it is positive and zero otherwise. However, it can suffer from the "dying ReLU" problem, where neurons become inactive and stop learning.
- **Leaky ReLU Function:** To address the dying ReLU issue, the leaky ReLU function was introduced. It allows a small, non-zero gradient for negative input values, ensuring neurons remain active and continue learning.
- **Softmax Function:** The softmax function is used in multi-class classification problems, as it converts a vector of input values into a probability distribution over multiple classes. It is commonly used in the output layer of a neural network.

Applications of Activation Functions

Activation functions are essential components of neural networks and significantly impact their performance. They are used in various applications, such as:

- **Image Recognition:** Convolutional Neural Networks (CNNs) use activation functions like ReLU to detect and classify objects within images.
- **Natural Language Processing:** Recurrent Neural Networks (RNNs) and Long Short-Term Memory (LSTM) networks use activation functions like tanh and sigmoid to process and generate text.
- **Reinforcement Learning:** Deep Q-Networks (DQNs) use activation functions like ReLU to learn optimal strategies for decision-making in complex environments.
- **Generative Adversarial Networks (GANs):** GANs use activation functions like Leaky ReLU to generate realistic images, music, and other creative outputs.

In conclusion, activation functions are vital elements in the design and performance of neural networks. By understanding their types and applications, coders can harness the power of AI and ML to create innovative solutions that tackle complex problems and shape the future of technology.

Training Techniques for Optimal Performance

In artificial intelligence and machine learning, training techniques are pivotal in achieving optimal performance for deep learning models and neural networks. As we delve into this section, we will explore various training techniques to help coders fine-tune their models and enhance their efficiency. By understanding and implementing these methods, developers can harness the full potential of AI and ML in their coding projects.

Gradient Descent and its Variants

Gradient descent is a fundamental optimization algorithm used to minimize the error or loss function in a neural network. It works by iteratively adjusting the model's parameters to find the optimal combination that minimizes the error. There are three primary variants of gradient descent:

- **Batch Gradient Descent:** This method computes the gradient of the entire dataset and updates the model's parameters accordingly. While it provides a stable convergence, it can be computationally expensive for large datasets.
- **Stochastic Gradient Descent (SGD):** Unlike batch gradient descent, SGD updates the model's parameters using only a single training example at a time. This approach is faster and can escape local minima but may result in a less stable convergence.
- **Mini-batch Gradient Descent:** This technique balances the previous two methods by updating the model's parameters using a small batch of training examples. It offers a good trade-off between computational efficiency and convergence stability.

Adaptive Learning Rate Techniques

Adaptive learning rate techniques adjust the learning rate during training, allowing the model to converge more quickly and accurately. Some popular adaptive learning rate methods include:

- **AdaGrad:** This method adapts the learning rate for each parameter based on the historical gradients, allowing for a more fine-tuned optimization.
- **RMSprop:** Similar to AdaGrad, RMSprop adjusts the learning rate for each parameter but uses an exponentially decaying average of squared gradients to prevent the learning rate from diminishing too quickly.

- **Adam (Adaptive Moment Estimation):** Combining the concepts of momentum and adaptive learning rates, Adam is a widely-used optimization algorithm that computes adaptive learning rates for each parameter while also considering the first and second moments of the gradients.

Regularization Techniques

Regularization techniques help prevent overfitting in neural networks by adding a penalty term to the loss function. This encourages the model to learn simpler and more generalizable patterns in the data. Common regularization techniques include:

- **L1 and L2 Regularization:** These methods add a penalty term proportional to the model's parameters' absolute value (L1) or the square (L2). This encourages the model to have smaller weights, reducing the risk of overfitting.
- **Dropout:** This technique randomly "drops out" a proportion of neurons during training, forcing the network to learn redundant representations and improving generalization.
- **Early Stopping:** By monitoring the model's performance on a validation set, early stopping halts the training process when the validation error starts to increase, preventing overfitting.

In conclusion, understanding and implementing these training techniques can significantly improve the performance of deep learning models and neural networks. By experimenting with various optimization algorithms, adaptive learning rates, and regularization methods, coders can fine-tune their AI and ML models to achieve optimal results. As we continue to explore the vast potential of deep learning and neural networks, these training techniques will undoubtedly play a crucial role in shaping the future of AI and ML in coding.

Real-World Applications of AI and ML in Coding

As we delve deeper into the fascinating world of artificial intelligence (AI) and machine learning (ML), it becomes increasingly evident that these technologies have the potential to revolutionize the way we approach coding and software development. In this section, we will explore some of the most promising real-world applications of AI and ML in coding, showcasing how these cutting-edge techniques are employed to solve complex problems, optimize performance, and create more efficient, intelligent systems.

Automated Code Generation and Optimization

One of the most exciting applications of AI and ML in coding is the ability to generate and optimize code automatically. By leveraging deep learning algorithms and neural networks, developers can create systems that analyze existing codebases, identify patterns and best practices, and generate new, optimized code based on these insights. This can significantly reduce the time and effort required to write and maintain code, allowing developers to focus on more strategic, high-level tasks.

Bug Detection and Resolution

AI and ML can also be employed to improve the bug detection and resolution process in software development. By training neural networks on large datasets of code with known issues, these systems can learn to identify potential bugs and vulnerabilities in new code. Moreover, AI-powered tools can suggest possible fixes for these issues, streamlining the debugging process and reducing the likelihood of human error.

Intelligent Code Completion

Another promising application of AI and ML in coding is the devel-

opment of intelligent code completion tools. These tools leverage natural language processing and machine learning algorithms to predict and suggest the most likely next line of code as a developer is typing. This can significantly speed up the coding process and help developers avoid common syntax errors and typos.

Code Review and Quality Assurance

Ensuring the quality and maintainability of code is a critical aspect of software development. AI and ML can automate and enhance the code review process by analyzing code for adherence to best practices, consistency, and potential performance issues. By providing developers with real-time feedback and suggestions for improvement, these tools can help maintain high-quality codebases and reduce the likelihood of technical debt.

Personalized Learning and Skill Development

As AI and ML continue to evolve, developers need to stay up-to-date with the latest techniques and best practices. AI-powered learning platforms can analyze a developer's existing skill set and recommend personalized learning paths, resources, and exercises to help them grow and stay competitive in the rapidly changing tech landscape.

In conclusion, integrating AI and ML into the coding process holds immense potential for improving efficiency, reducing errors, and fostering innovation in software development. As these technologies continue to advance, we can expect to see even more groundbreaking applications emerge, further transforming the way we approach coding and shaping the future of the software development industry.

The Future of Deep Learning and Neural Networks

As we reach the end of this enlightening journey through the world of artificial intelligence and machine learning, it is essential to take a moment to reflect on the incredible advancements that have been made in the field of deep learning and neural networks. The potential of these technologies is immense, and their coding applications are only beginning to be explored. In this conclusion, we will discuss the future of deep learning and neural networks and how they will continue to shape the world of coding and beyond.

The rapid progress in deep learning and neural networks has been astounding. From their humble beginnings as simple models of the human brain, these powerful tools have evolved into complex systems capable of solving some of the most challenging problems in computer science. As we continue to push the boundaries of what is possible with AI and ML, it is clear that deep learning and neural networks will play a central role in shaping the future of coding.

One of the most exciting aspects of deep learning and neural networks is their ability to learn and adapt. As these systems become more sophisticated, they can tackle increasingly complex tasks, making them invaluable tools for coders. In the future, we expect to see AI and ML integrated into a wide range of applications, from software development and data analysis to cybersecurity and natural language processing.

Furthermore, developing new neural network architectures and activation functions will continue to drive innovation in the field. As researchers and engineers experiment with novel approaches, we expect to see more powerful and efficient models emerge. These advancements will improve the performance of existing applications and open up new possibilities for AI and ML in coding.

In addition to these technical advancements, the future of deep learning and neural networks will also be shaped by the ethical considerations surrounding their use. As AI and ML become more prevalent daily, we must develop a robust ethical framework to guide their development and deployment. This will ensure that these powerful tools are used responsibly and for the benefit of all.

Finally, the future of deep learning and neural networks will be characterized by increased collaboration between researchers, engineers, and coders. As the field continues to grow and evolve, we must foster cooperation and knowledge-sharing. By working together, we can unlock the full potential of AI and ML and create a brighter future for coding and beyond.

In conclusion, the future of deep learning and neural networks is incredibly promising. As these technologies continue to advance, they will revolutionize the world of coding, opening up new possibilities and transforming how we approach problem-solving. By embracing the power of AI and ML, we can look forward to a future where coding is more efficient, effective, and accessible than ever before.

Chapter Summary

- Deep learning, a subset of machine learning, uses artificial neural networks inspired by the human brain to process and analyze vast amounts of data, making them indispensable in various applications such as natural language processing and computer vision.
- Neural network architectures, including feedforward networks, recurrent networks, and convolutional networks, play a crucial role in determining the performance and capabilities of deep learning models.
- Activation functions, such as sigmoid, ReLU, and softmax, introduce non-linearity into neural networks, allowing them to learn complex patterns and relationships in the data.
- Training techniques, including gradient descent, backpropagation, and regularization, are essential for achieving optimal performance in deep learning models.
- Real-world applications of AI and ML in coding include automated code generation, bug detection and resolution, intelligent code completion, code review and quality assurance, and personalized learning and skill development.
- The future of deep learning and neural networks will be shaped by advancements in neural network architectures, activation functions, and ethical considerations surrounding their use.

- Increased collaboration between researchers, engineers, and coders will be essential for unlocking the full potential of AI and ML in coding and beyond.
- As deep learning and neural networks continue to advance, they will revolutionize the world of coding, making it more efficient, practical, and accessible than ever before.

8

NATURAL LANGUAGE PROCESSING: TEXT ANALYSIS, SENTIMENT ANALYSIS, AND CHATBOTS

I n the rapidly shifting domain of artificial intelligence (AI) and machine learning (ML), one area that has garnered significant attention and growth is Natural Language Processing (NLP). As coders, it is essential to understand the fundamentals of NLP and its applications to stay ahead in the game and create innovative solutions for a wide range of industries. In this chapter, we will delve into the fascinating realm of NLP, exploring text analysis, sentiment analysis, and chatbots while also discussing how to integrate AI and ML into your NLP projects.

At its core, natural language processing is the intersection of computer science, AI, and linguistics. It focuses on enabling computers to understand, interpret, and generate human language in a meaningful and helpful way. This is no small feat, as human language is incredibly complex, filled with nuances, idioms, and context-dependent meanings. However, the advancements in AI and ML have made it possible for computers to process and analyze large volumes of text, opening up a world of possibilities for coders.

As a coder, you might wonder why NLP is relevant to you. The answer lies in the vast array of applications to which NLP techniques can be applied. From sentiment analysis that helps businesses understand customer feedback to chatbots that provide seamless customer support, NLP is revolutionizing how we interact with technology. By incorporating NLP into your skillset, you will be better equipped to create cutting-edge applications that cater to the growing demand for intelligent and intuitive systems.

In the following sections, we will explore various NLP techniques and their applications, starting with text analysis. Text analysis is the foundation of NLP, which involves breaking down and understanding language structure. This knowledge can then be applied to more advanced NLP tasks, such as sentiment analysis, which aims to decipher the emotions and opinions expressed in a piece of text. Finally, we will discuss chatbots and how they utilize NLP to engage in meaningful conversations with users.

As we journey through the world of Natural Language Processing, you will gain valuable insights into the power of AI and ML in transforming how we interact with technology. By the end of this chapter, you will have a solid understanding of NLP and its applications, empowering you to create innovative solutions that harness the power of language and communication. So, let's embark on this exciting adventure and discover the limitless potential of Natural Language Processing for coders.

Text Analysis Techniques and Applications

This section will delve into the fascinating world of text analysis, exploring various techniques and their applications in artificial intelligence and machine learning. As coders, understanding these methods will enable you to harness the power of natural language processing (NLP) to create innovative solutions and enhance user experiences.

Tokenization and Text Preprocessing

The first step in text analysis is breaking down the text into smaller units, known as tokens. Tokenization is converting a text sequence into individual words, phrases, symbols, or other meaningful elements. This technique allows for easier manipulation and analysis of the text data.

Text preprocessing is another crucial aspect of text analysis. It involves cleaning and transforming raw text data into a structured format that machine learning algorithms can easily understand. Common preprocessing tasks include:

- **Lowercasing:** Converting all text to lowercase to ensure uniformity.
- **Removing special characters and numbers:** Eliminating any irrelevant elements that may hinder analysis.
- **Stopword removal:** Filtering out common words (e.g., 'and', 'the', 'is') that do not contribute to the meaning of the text.
- **Stemming and Lemmatization:** Reducing words to their root form to consolidate similar terms and reduce dimensionality.

Feature Extraction and Representation

Once the text data is preprocessed, the next step is to extract relevant features and represent them in a format that can be fed into machine learning models. Two popular techniques for feature extraction and representation are:

- **Bag of Words (BoW):** This approach represents text data as a 'bag' (unordered set) of its words, disregarding grammar and word order but keeping track of frequency. Each document is represented as a vector, with the length of the vector being the total number of unique words in the corpus (collection of documents). The value at each position in the vector indicates the frequency of the corresponding word in the document.
- **Term Frequency-Inverse Document Frequency (TF-IDF):** This method is an extension of the BoW approach, taking into account the frequency of a word in a document and its importance across the entire corpus. The idea is to give higher weight to words more specific to a particular document and lower weight to words common across documents.

Text Classification and Clustering

With the text data preprocessed and represented in a suitable format, we can now apply machine learning algorithms to perform various tasks, such as:

- **Text Classification:** Assigning predefined categories (labels) to a given text based on its content. Typical applications include spam detection, sentiment analysis, and topic identification. Popular algorithms for text classification include Naive Bayes, Support Vector Machines, and Deep Learning models such as Convolutional Neural Networks (CNNs) and Recurrent Neural Networks (RNNs).
- **Text Clustering:** Grouping similar text documents based on their content without any prior knowledge of categories or labels. This unsupervised learning technique is helpful for

discovering hidden patterns and structures in the data. Standard algorithms for text clustering include K-means, Hierarchical Clustering, and Latent Dirichlet Allocation (LDA).

In conclusion, text analysis techniques play a vital role in harnessing the power of NLP for various AI and ML applications. By understanding and implementing these methods, coders can unlock new possibilities and create innovative solutions that leverage the vast potential of natural language data.

Sentiment Analysis: Understanding Emotions in Text

In today's digital age, understanding and interpreting human emotions in text has become increasingly important. Sentiment analysis, also known as opinion mining or emotion AI, is a subfield of natural language processing (NLP) that focuses on identifying and extracting subjective information from textual data. This section will delve into sentiment analysis, exploring its techniques, applications, and significance for coders working with AI and ML.

The Basics of Sentiment Analysis

Sentiment analysis aims to determine the sentiment or emotion behind a piece of text, be it positive, negative, or neutral. This can be achieved through various techniques, including machine learning, lexicon-based approaches, and deep learning. The primary goal is to gain insights into the opinions and emotions expressed by users, which can be invaluable for businesses, researchers, and developers alike.

Techniques for Sentiment Analysis

- **Machine Learning:** Supervised machine learning algorithms, such as Naïve Bayes, Support Vector Machines (SVM), and Decision Trees, can be trained on labeled datasets to classify text based on sentiment. These algorithms learn from the input data and make predictions based on patterns and relationships they identify.

- **Lexicon-Based Approaches:** This technique relies on predefined sentiment lexicons, lists of words, and phrases associated with specific emotions or sentiments. The overall sentiment can be determined by analyzing the frequency and context of these words in a given text.
- **Deep Learning:** Neural networks, such as Convolutional Neural Networks (CNN) and Recurrent Neural Networks (RNN), can capture complex patterns and relationships in textual data. These models can be particularly effective in handling large datasets and understanding the nuances of human language.

Applications of Sentiment Analysis

- **Social Media Monitoring:** Sentiment analysis can be used to track public opinion on social media platforms, helping businesses and organizations understand how the audience perceives their products, services, or campaigns.
- **Customer Feedback Analysis:** By analyzing customer reviews and feedback, businesses can identify areas of improvement, address customer concerns, and enhance their overall customer experience.
- **Market Research:** Sentiment analysis can provide valuable insights into market trends and consumer preferences, enabling businesses to make informed decisions and stay ahead of the competition.
- **Political Analysis:** By gauging public sentiment on political issues, candidates, and campaigns, sentiment analysis can help predict election outcomes and inform political strategies.

The Role of Coders in Sentiment Analysis

As AI and ML advance, the demand for skilled coders in sentiment analysis will only grow. Coders play a crucial role in developing and refining algorithms, creating and maintaining sentiment lexicons, and integrating sentiment analysis tools into various applications. By staying up-to-date with the latest techniques and developments in NLP, coders can contribute to the evolution of sentiment analysis and its impact on industries worldwide.

In conclusion, sentiment analysis is a powerful tool for understanding emotions in text, with numerous applications across various domains. As a coder working with AI and ML, mastering sentiment analysis techniques and staying informed about the latest advancements in NLP will enhance your skillset and open doors to exciting opportunities in this rapidly evolving field.

Building Chatbots: Conversational AI and User Interaction

Chatbots have become a powerful tool for businesses and developers in today's fast-paced digital world. These intelligent virtual assistants are designed to interact with users through natural language processing (NLP), providing a seamless and efficient communication experience. This section will delve into the fascinating world of chatbots, exploring the underlying technology, user interaction, and the steps to build your own conversational AI.

The Essence of Chatbots

At their core, chatbots are AI-driven programs that can understand, interpret, and respond to human language. They can be integrated into various platforms, such as websites, messaging apps, or even social media, to provide instant support, answer queries, or engage users in conversation. The primary goal of chatbots is to mimic human-like interactions, making them an invaluable asset in enhancing user experience and customer satisfaction.

Conversational AI: The Driving Force Behind Chatbots

Conversational AI is the technology that enables chatbots to understand and process human language. It combines NLP, machine learning (ML), and artificial intelligence (AI) to analyze text or speech input, extract meaning, and generate appropriate responses. This intricate process involves several steps, including tokenization, parsing, and entity recognition, which help the chatbot comprehend the user's intent and respond accordingly.

User Interaction: The Key to Successful Chatbots

For a chatbot to be effective, it must be able to engage users naturally and intuitively. This involves understanding the context of the conversation, providing relevant information, and maintaining a consistent tone. To achieve this, developers must focus on the following aspects:

- **Personalization:** Tailoring the chatbot's responses to the user's preferences and needs can significantly enhance the interaction experience. This can be achieved by analyzing user data, such as browsing history or previous interactions, to provide personalized recommendations or support.
- **Context-awareness:** Chatbots should be able to understand the context of the conversation and respond accordingly. This may involve maintaining the conversation history, recognizing user emotions, or detecting sarcasm to ensure appropriate responses.
- **Natural language generation:** Crafting human-like responses is crucial for a chatbot's success. This can be achieved through natural language generation (NLG), which involves converting structured data into coherent and engaging text.

Building Your Own Chatbot: A Step-by-Step Guide

1. **Define the purpose:** Before diving into the development process, it is essential to identify the primary goal of your chatbot. This could range from customer support to product recommendations or even entertainment.

2. **Choose a platform:** Select a suitable platform for your chatbot, such as Facebook Messenger, Slack, or your own website. This decision will influence the development process and the tools you will need.

3. **Design the conversation flow:** Map out the potential conversation paths, including user inputs, chatbot responses, and fallback options for unrecognized queries.

4. **Develop the NLP model:** Utilize NLP libraries and frameworks, such as TensorFlow or spaCy, to build your chatbot's underlying language processing model.

5. **Train and test the chatbot:** Use a dataset of sample conversations to train your chatbot and evaluate its performance. Continuously refine the model to improve its accuracy and responsiveness.

6. **Integrate and deploy:** Once your chatbot is ready, integrate it into the chosen platform and monitor its performance. Gather user feedback and make necessary adjustments to enhance the overall experience.

In conclusion, chatbots have revolutionized how businesses and users interact, offering a more personalized and efficient communication channel. By understanding the intricacies of conversational AI and user interaction, developers can harness the power of NLP, AI, and ML to create engaging and effective chatbots that cater to a wide range of applications. As technology advances, the potential for natural language processing and its impact on coders is limitless, opening up new avenues for innovation and growth.

Integrating AI and ML into Your NLP Projects

As we delve deeper into the fascinating world of Natural Language Processing (NLP), it becomes increasingly evident that the integration of Artificial Intelligence (AI) and Machine Learning (ML) is crucial for the development of advanced NLP projects. In this section, we will explore the process of incorporating AI and ML techniques into your NLP projects, enabling you to create more sophisticated and efficient applications.

Identifying the Problem and Setting Goals

Before diving into the technical aspects of AI and ML integration, it is essential to identify the specific problem you aim to solve with your NLP project. This involves defining clear objectives and determining the desired outcomes. For instance, you may want to create a sentiment analysis tool that accurately gauges customer opinions on a product or service, or you may want to develop a chatbot capable of providing personalized recommendations to users.

Selecting the Right AI and ML Techniques

Once you have established your project's goals, the next step is choosing the appropriate AI and ML techniques to help you achieve those objectives. Various algorithms and models are available, each with strengths and weaknesses. Some popular techniques include:

- **Supervised Learning:** This approach involves training a model using labeled data, where the input-output pairs are known. Supervised learning is particularly useful for text classification and sentiment analysis tasks.
- **Unsupervised Learning:** In this method, the model learns from unlabeled data by identifying patterns and structures within the dataset. Unsupervised learning is often employed for tasks like topic modeling and clustering.

- **Deep Learning:** This subset of ML involves using artificial neural networks to model complex patterns in data. Deep learning techniques, such as recurrent neural networks (RNNs) and transformers, have proven highly effective in various NLP tasks, including machine translation and text generation.

Preprocessing and Feature Engineering

To ensure the success of your AI and ML integration, it is vital to preprocess your text data and extract relevant features. This process typically involves cleaning and tokenizing the text, removing stop words, and stemming or lemmatizing words to reduce them to their root forms. Additionally, you may need to convert the text into numerical representations, such as word embeddings or bag-of-words representations, which ML algorithms can efficiently process.

Model Training and Evaluation

You can train your model after preprocessing your data and selecting the appropriate AI and ML techniques. This involves feeding the processed data into the chosen algorithm and adjusting the model's parameters to minimize the error between the predicted and actual outputs. Evaluating your model's performance using various metrics, such as accuracy, precision, recall, and F1 score, is crucial to ensure that it meets your project's objectives.

Fine-tuning and Optimization

Once your model has been trained and evaluated, you may need to fine-tune its parameters or optimize its architecture to improve its performance further. This process may involve adjusting hyperparameters, employing regularization techniques to prevent overfitting, or exploring more advanced AI and ML techniques, such as transfer learning or ensemble methods.

In conclusion, integrating AI and ML into your NLP projects can significantly enhance their capabilities and efficiency. By following the steps outlined in this section, you will be well-equipped to develop cutting-edge NLP applications that harness the power of AI and ML, ultimately shaping the future of language processing and its impact on coders.

The Future of Natural Language Processing and Its Impact on Coders

As we reach the end of this enlightening journey through the world of Natural Language Processing (NLP), it is essential to take a moment to reflect on the future of this rapidly evolving field and its impact on coders. Artificial Intelligence (AI) and Machine Learning (ML) advancements have already transformed how we interact with technology, and NLP is at the forefront of this revolution.

In the coming years, we can expect NLP to become even more sophisticated and versatile, enabling machines to understand and process human language with unprecedented accuracy. This will open up many opportunities for coders, who will be instrumental in shaping the future of NLP and its applications.

One of the most significant growth areas in NLP will be the development of more advanced and intuitive chatbots. As conversational AI continues to improve, chatbots will become increasingly capable of understanding complex language patterns and providing more accurate and personalized responses. This will lead to a higher demand for skilled coders who can design, develop, and maintain these intelligent systems.

Moreover, integrating AI and ML into NLP projects will become more seamless, allowing coders to harness the power of these technologies more efficiently. This will result in the creation of more advanced tools and applications for text analysis, sentiment analysis, and other NLP tasks. Consequently, coders must stay up-to-date with the latest developments in AI and ML to remain competitive in the job market.

Another exciting prospect for the future of NLP is the potential for cross-disciplinary collaboration. As NLP techniques become more refined, they will be increasingly applied to various fields, such as healthcare, finance, and education. This will create new opportunities for coders to work alongside professionals from diverse backgrounds, fostering innovation and driving progress in multiple domains.

Furthermore, as NLP evolves, ethical considerations will become increasingly important. Coders must be mindful of the potential biases and ethical implications of the algorithms they develop, ensuring that their work promotes fairness and inclusivity. This will require a deep understanding of NLP's technical and social aspects, highlighting the importance of a well-rounded education for aspiring coders.

In conclusion, the future of Natural Language Processing is undoubtedly bright, and its impact on coders will be profound. As NLP techniques become more advanced and widespread, coders will play a crucial role in shaping how we communicate with machines and unlocking the full potential of AI and ML. By staying informed about the latest developments in NLP and honing their skills, coders will be well-equipped to navigate this exciting and ever-changing landscape.

Chapter Summary

- Natural Language Processing (NLP) is the intersection of computer science, AI, and linguistics, focusing on enabling computers to understand, interpret, and generate human language meaningfully and usefully.
- Text analysis is the foundation of NLP, involving techniques such as tokenization, text preprocessing, feature extraction, and representation, which can be applied to more advanced NLP tasks like sentiment analysis and chatbots.
- Sentiment analysis, a subfield of NLP, focuses on identifying and extracting subjective information from textual data, helping businesses understand customer feedback, monitor social media, and conduct market research.

- Powered by conversational AI, chatbots are intelligent virtual assistants designed to interact with users through NLP, providing seamless and efficient communication experiences across various platforms.
- Integrating AI and ML into NLP projects involves identifying the problem, selecting the right techniques, preprocessing and feature engineering, model training and evaluation, and fine-tuning and optimization.
- The future of NLP will see more advanced and intuitive chatbots, seamless integration of AI and ML, and cross-disciplinary collaboration, creating new opportunities for coders in various fields.
- Ethical considerations will become increasingly important in NLP, with coders needing to be mindful of potential biases and ethical implications of the algorithms they develop.
- As NLP continues to evolve, coders must stay up-to-date with the latest developments in AI and ML to remain competitive in the job market and contribute to the growth of NLP applications.

9

COMPUTER VISION AND IMAGE RECOGNITION: CONVOLUTIONAL NEURAL NETWORKS AND OBJECT DETECTION

I n the dynamic and changing sphere of artificial intelligence (AI) and machine learning (ML), computer vision and image recognition have emerged as two of the most fascinating and rapidly growing subfields. These technologies can revolutionize various industries, from healthcare and agriculture to security and entertainment. This chapter will delve into the intricacies of computer vision and image recognition, exploring the underlying concepts, techniques, and applications that make these technologies so powerful and transformative.

Computer vision is a multidisciplinary field that aims to enable computers to interpret and understand the visual world, much like humans do. By processing and analyzing digital images and videos, computer vision algorithms can extract valuable information, recognize patterns, and make intelligent decisions based on the visual data. This ability to "see" and comprehend the world around us has far-reaching implications, as it can significantly enhance the capabilities of AI and ML systems across various domains.

Image recognition, a subset of computer vision, focuses on identifying and classifying objects within images. This process involves detecting specific features, such as shapes, colors, and textures, and using them to distinguish between different objects or categories. The ultimate goal of image recognition is to teach machines to recognize and understand images' content, enabling them to perform tasks that were once exclusive to human perception.

One of the most groundbreaking advancements in computer vision and image recognition has been the development of Convolutional Neural Networks (CNNs). These deep learning models have demonstrated remarkable success in various image recognition tasks, outperforming traditional methods and setting new benchmarks in the field. In this chapter, we will explore the architecture and applications of CNNs and other object detection techniques that have shaped the landscape of computer vision.

As we journey through the world of computer vision and image recognition, we will also examine real-world applications and case studies that showcase the transformative power of these technologies. From self-driving cars and facial recognition systems to medical imaging and wildlife conservation, computer vision and image recognition are poised to redefine how we live, work, and interact with our environment.

Finally, we will discuss the future of computer vision and image recognition in AI and ML, highlighting the challenges, opportunities, and emerging trends shaping the next generation of intelligent systems. As we continue to push the boundaries of what machines can see and understand, there is no doubt that computer vision and image recognition will play a pivotal role in the evolution of AI and ML, unlocking new possibilities and transforming the world as we know it.

Exploring Convolutional Neural Networks: Architecture and Applications

In artificial intelligence and machine learning, computer vision has emerged as a powerful tool for enabling computers to perceive and interpret visual information from the world. At the heart of this revolution lies the Convolutional Neural Network (CNN), a class of deep learning models specifically designed for image recognition and analysis. In this section, we will delve into the architecture and applications of CNNs, shedding light on their remarkable capabilities and potential impact on computer vision.

The Architecture of Convolutional Neural Networks

Convolutional Neural Networks are artificial neural networks that have been explicitly tailored for processing grid-like data structures, such as images. The architecture of a CNN is composed of several interconnected layers, each designed to perform a specific function in the image recognition process. These layers can be broadly categorized into convolutional layers, pooling layers, and fully connected layers.

- **Convolutional Layers:** The primary building blocks of a CNN, convolutional layers detect local features within an image, such as edges, corners, and textures. They achieve this by applying a series of filters, or kernels, to the input image, which results in a set of feature maps. These feature maps represent the presence of specific features at different locations within the image.

- **Pooling Layers:** Following the convolutional layers, pooling layers reduce the spatial dimensions of the feature maps, effectively summarizing the information contained within them. This process, known as downsampling, helps to reduce the computational complexity of the network and improve its robustness to small variations in the input data.
- **Fully Connected Layers:** In the final stage of a CNN's architecture, fully connected layers integrate the information extracted by the preceding convolutional and pooling layers. These layers are responsible for producing the network's final output, which typically takes the form of a probability distribution over the possible classes or objects present in the input image.

Applications of Convolutional Neural Networks

The unique architecture of CNNs has made them particularly well-suited for a wide range of computer vision tasks. Some of the most notable applications of CNNs include:

- **Image Classification:** Perhaps the most fundamental application of CNNs, image classification involves assigning an input image to one of several predefined categories. CNNs have demonstrated remarkable success in this domain, achieving state-of-the-art performance on benchmark datasets such as ImageNet.
- **Object Detection:** Building upon the capabilities of image classification, object detection tasks require CNNs to identify the objects present in an image and localize them within the image frame. This is typically achieved by predicting bounding boxes around the detected objects and their corresponding class labels.
- **Semantic Segmentation:** In semantic segmentation tasks, CNNs assign a class label to each pixel in an input image, effectively partitioning the image into distinct regions

corresponding to different objects or scene elements. This level of granularity enables a more detailed understanding of the image content and has applications in areas such as autonomous vehicles and robotics.

- **Image Generation and Style Transfer:** CNNs have also been utilized for creative purposes, such as generating new images or transferring the artistic style of one image onto another. This is achieved through generative models, such as Generative Adversarial Networks (GANs), which leverage the feature extraction capabilities of CNNs to synthesize visually compelling images.

In conclusion, Convolutional Neural Networks have emerged as a cornerstone of modern computer vision, enabling machines to perceive and interpret visual information with unprecedented accuracy and efficiency. As we continue to explore the potential of CNNs in various applications, it is clear that their impact on the field of AI and ML will be both profound and far-reaching.

Object Detection Techniques: From Traditional Methods to Deep Learning Approaches

The realm of object detection has witnessed a remarkable evolution over the years, transitioning from traditional methods to deep learning approaches. In this section, we will delve into the intricacies of these techniques, highlighting their strengths and limitations and exploring how they have shaped the landscape of computer vision and image recognition.

Traditional Object Detection Methods

Before the advent of deep learning, computer vision researchers relied on traditional methods for object detection. These techniques typically involved feature extraction and applying machine learning algorithms to classify objects. Some of the most prominent traditional methods include:

- **Viola-Jones Algorithm:** This groundbreaking method, introduced in 2001, employed Haar-like features and a cascaded classifier to detect objects, particularly faces, in real time. The Viola-Jones algorithm's success can be attributed to its speed and efficiency, which paved the way for further advancements in object detection.
- **Scale-Invariant Feature Transform (SIFT):** SIFT is a robust feature extraction technique that identifies key points and their corresponding descriptors in an image. These features are invariant to scale, rotation, and illumination changes, making SIFT suitable for various object recognition tasks.
- **Histogram of Oriented Gradients (HOG):** HOG is another popular feature extraction method that captures the distribution of gradients and edge directions in an image. It has been widely used for pedestrian detection and other object recognition applications.

Despite their contributions to the field, traditional object detection methods have certain limitations. They often struggle with variations in object appearance, occlusions, and complex backgrounds. Moreover, these techniques require manual feature engineering, which can be time-consuming and may not always yield optimal results.

Deep Learning Approaches to Object Detection

The emergence of deep learning has revolutionized object detection, offering improved accuracy and efficiency. Convolutional Neural Networks (CNNs) have been at the forefront of this transformation, with several architectures and techniques being developed to tackle object detection tasks. Some of the most notable deep learning approaches include:

- **Region-based CNNs (R-CNN):** R-CNNs combine the power of CNNs with region proposal methods to detect objects in an image. The R-CNN framework generates region proposals, extracts feature using a CNN, and classifies objects using a support vector machine (SVM) classifier. Variants of R-CNN, such as Fast R-CNN and Faster R-CNN, have been developed to address the computational inefficiencies of the original R-CNN.
- **You Only Look Once (YOLO):** YOLO is a real-time object detection system that frames object detection as a single regression problem. It divides the input image into a grid and predicts bounding boxes and class probabilities for each grid cell. YOLO's end-to-end architecture allows for faster processing and real-time detection.
- **Single Shot MultiBox Detector (SSD):** SSD is another real-time object detection technique that eliminates the need for region proposals. It predicts bounding boxes and class probabilities directly from feature maps at different scales, resulting in a more efficient and accurate detection process.

Deep learning approaches have significantly outperformed traditional methods in object detection tasks thanks to their ability to learn hierarchical features automatically. These techniques have proven more robust and adaptable, handling relative ease variations in object appearance, occlusions, and complex backgrounds.

In conclusion, the transition from traditional methods to deep learning approaches has been instrumental in advancing the field of object detection. As we continue to explore the potential of AI and ML for coders, it is crucial to understand and appreciate the techniques that have shaped the landscape of computer vision and image recognition. The future of this domain promises even more exciting developments as researchers and practitioners strive to push the boundaries of what is possible with AI and ML.

Implementing Convolutional Neural Networks for Image Recognition Tasks

This section delves into the practical aspects of implementing Convolutional Neural Networks (CNNs) for image recognition tasks. We will discuss the essential components of a CNN, the process of building a model, and the tools and frameworks available for coders to develop and deploy these networks efficiently.

Essential Components of a Convolutional Neural Network

A typical CNN consists of several layers, each designed to perform a specific function in the image recognition process. These layers include:

- **Input Layer:** This layer receives the input image and preprocesses it to a suitable format for further processing. Preprocessing may involve resizing, normalization, and data augmentation techniques.
- **Convolutional Layer:** The core component of a CNN, the convolutional layer applies a series of filters to the input image, detecting various features such as edges, corners, and textures. These filters, also known as kernels, slide over the image and perform element-wise multiplication, generating feature maps.
- **Activation Layer:** Following the convolutional layer, the activation layer introduces non-linearity into the network by applying an activation function, such as the Rectified Linear Unit (ReLU), to the feature maps. This step enhances the network's ability to learn complex patterns.
- **Pooling Layer:** The pooling layer reduces the spatial dimensions of the feature maps, thereby decreasing computational complexity and preventing overfitting. Common pooling techniques include max pooling and average pooling.

- **Fully Connected Layer:** After several iterations of convolutional, activation, and pooling layers, the fully connected layer flattens the feature maps into a single vector. This vector is then fed into a classifier, such as a softmax function, to generate the final output probabilities for each class.

Building a Convolutional Neural Network Model

To implement a CNN for image recognition tasks, follow these general steps:

1. **Data Preparation:** Collect and preprocess a dataset of labeled images. Split the dataset into training, validation, and testing sets.
2. **Model Architecture:** Design the CNN architecture by stacking the appropriate layers in a sequential manner. Determine the number of filters, kernel sizes, and other hyperparameters based on the specific problem and dataset.
3. **Model Training:** Train the CNN using the training set, adjusting the weights and biases through backpropagation and optimization algorithms such as stochastic gradient descent. Monitor the model's performance on the validation set to prevent overfitting and fine-tune hyperparameters.
4. **Model Evaluation:** Assess the trained CNN's performance on the testing set using accuracy, precision, recall, and F1 score metrics.
5. **Model Deployment:** Integrate the trained CNN into an application or system for real-time image recognition tasks.

Tools and Frameworks for Implementing Convolutional Neural Networks

Several tools and frameworks are available to facilitate the implementation of CNNs for image recognition tasks. Some popular options include:

- **TensorFlow:** An open-source machine learning library developed by Google, TensorFlow offers a comprehensive ecosystem for building, training, and deploying CNNs.
- **Keras:** A high-level neural networks API, Keras simplifies the process of building and training CNNs by providing an intuitive interface and pre-built layers. Keras can run on top of TensorFlow, Microsoft Cognitive Toolkit, or Theano.
- **PyTorch:** Developed by Facebook's AI Research lab, PyTorch is a flexible and efficient deep learning framework that supports dynamic computation graphs, making it particularly suitable for research purposes.
- **Caffe:** A deep learning framework developed by the Berkeley Vision and Learning Center, Caffe is specifically designed for image recognition tasks and offers a fast and efficient implementation of CNNs.

In conclusion, implementing Convolutional Neural Networks for image recognition tasks involves understanding the essential components, building and training the model, and utilizing the appropriate tools and frameworks. As AI and ML continue to advance, we can expect further improvements in the accuracy and efficiency of CNNs, paving the way for more sophisticated and diverse applications in computer vision.

Real-World Applications and Case Studies in Computer Vision

The advancements in artificial intelligence (AI) and machine learning (ML) have significantly impacted various industries, with computer vision and image recognition playing a crucial role in this transformation. In this section, we will delve into real-world applications and case studies that demonstrate the power of computer vision and image recognition in solving complex problems and enhancing our daily lives.

Healthcare and Medical Imaging

One of the most promising applications of computer vision lies in the healthcare industry, particularly in medical imaging. By leveraging convolutional neural networks (CNNs) and other deep learning techniques, computer vision algorithms can analyze medical images, such as X-rays, MRIs, and CT scans, to accurately detect and diagnose diseases. For instance, researchers have developed AI models to identify early signs of diabetic retinopathy, lung cancer, and Alzheimer's disease, enabling timely intervention and treatment.

Autonomous Vehicles

Integrating computer vision and image recognition technologies has revolutionized the automotive industry. Self-driving cars rely heavily on these techniques to navigate safely and efficiently. CNNs process and analyze data from cameras, LiDAR, and other sensors, allowing the vehicle to recognize and track objects like pedestrians, other vehicles, and traffic signs. This real-time object detection and tracking capability is essential for autonomous vehicles to make informed decisions and avoid accidents.

Retail and E-commerce

Computer vision has also found its way into the retail and e-commerce sectors, enhancing customer experiences and streamlining operations. For example, image recognition algorithms can analyze customer preferences and shopping habits, enabling retailers to offer personalized product recommendations. Additionally, computer vision-powered checkout systems can automatically identify and track items, reducing the need for manual barcode scanning and speeding up the checkout process.

Agriculture and Precision Farming

The agriculture industry has benefited from adopting computer vision and image recognition technologies, leading to the emergence of precision farming. By analyzing images captured by drones or satellites, AI algorithms can identify crop health, monitor growth, and detect signs of pests or diseases. This information allows farmers to make data-driven decisions, optimize resource usage, and improve crop yields.

Surveillance and Security

Computer vision plays a vital role in enhancing security and surveillance systems. Advanced image recognition algorithms can analyze real-time video feeds, detecting and tracking suspicious activities, such as unattended bags, trespassing, or loitering. Furthermore, facial recognition technology has become increasingly prevalent in various security applications, from unlocking smartphones to identifying criminals in public spaces.

In conclusion, the real-world applications and case studies discussed in this section highlight the immense potential of computer vision and image recognition in transforming industries and improving our daily lives. As AI and ML evolve, we can expect even more innovative and impactful use cases for these technologies.

The Future of Computer Vision and Image Recognition in AI and ML

As we reach the end of our exploration into the fascinating world of computer vision and image recognition, we must take a step back and consider the potential future developments in this field. The rapid advancements in artificial intelligence (AI) and machine learning (ML) have already transformed how we interact with technology, and the impact of these innovations on computer vision is no exception.

In this concluding section, we will delve into the possible future trajectories of computer vision and image recognition, highlighting the potential breakthroughs and challenges. By understanding the direction in which this technology is headed, we can better prepare ourselves for the exciting opportunities in AI and ML.

One of the most promising areas of development in computer vision is the continued improvement of convolutional neural networks (CNNs) and other deep learning techniques. We expect to see even more accurate and efficient image recognition systems as researchers refine these algorithms. This will enable a wide range of applications, from autonomous vehicles to advanced medical diagnostics, to become increasingly sophisticated and reliable.

Another exciting prospect for the future of computer vision is integrating other sensory data, such as audio and touch, to create more comprehensive and intuitive AI systems. By combining multiple sources of information, these systems can better understand and interpret the world around them, leading to more accurate and versatile applications.

In addition to these technological advancements, the future of computer vision will also be shaped by ethical considerations. As AI and ML systems become more prevalent in our daily lives, it is crucial to ensure that they are designed and implemented to respect privacy, fairness, and transparency. This will require ongoing collaboration between researchers, policymakers, and industry leaders to establish best practices and guidelines for the responsible development and deployment of computer vision technologies.

Finally, the future of computer vision and image recognition will be heavily influenced by the availability of high-quality, diverse datasets. As AI and ML systems rely on vast amounts of data to learn and improve, ensuring that these datasets represent a diverse range of human experiences and perspectives is essential. This will not only lead to more accurate and effective AI systems but also help mitigate potential biases and promote fairness in developing and deploying these technologies.

In conclusion, the future of computer vision and image recognition in AI and ML has exciting possibilities and challenges. As we continue to push the boundaries of what is possible with these technologies, it is essential to remain mindful of the ethical implications and strive to create AI systems that are not only powerful but also responsible and inclusive. By doing so, we can unlock the full potential of computer vision and image recognition, transforming how we live, work, and interact with the world around us.

Chapter Summary

- Computer vision and image recognition are rapidly growing subfields of AI and ML, with the potential to revolutionize various industries, such as healthcare, agriculture, security, and entertainment.
- Convolutional Neural Networks (CNNs) are deep learning models specifically designed for image recognition tasks, consisting of convolutional layers, pooling layers, and fully connected layers.
- CNNs have demonstrated remarkable success in various image recognition tasks, including image classification, object detection, semantic segmentation, image generation, and style transfer.
- Object detection techniques have evolved from traditional methods like Viola-Jones Algorithm, SIFT, and HOG to deep learning approaches like R-CNN, YOLO, and SSD.
- Implementing CNNs for image recognition tasks involves understanding the essential components, building and training the model, and utilizing appropriate tools and frameworks like TensorFlow, Keras, PyTorch, and Caffe.
- Real-world applications of computer vision and image recognition include healthcare and medical imaging, autonomous vehicles, retail and e-commerce, agriculture and precision farming, and surveillance and security.
- The future of computer vision and image recognition will likely see continued improvement of CNNs, integration of

other sensory data, addressing ethical considerations, and ensuring the availability of high-quality, diverse datasets.

- As AI and ML continue to evolve, it is crucial to remain mindful of the ethical implications and strive to create AI systems that are not only powerful but also responsible and inclusive, unlocking the full potential of computer vision and image recognition.

10

ETHICAL CONSIDERATIONS AND RESPONSIBLE AI DEVELOPMENT

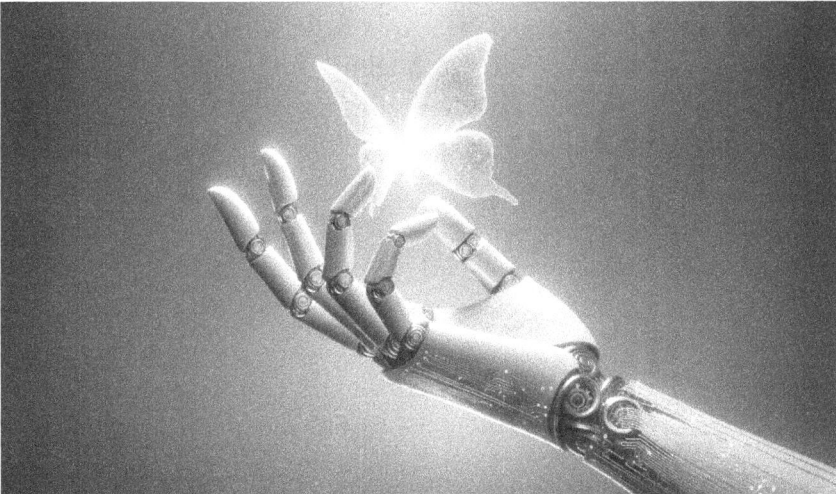

I
n today's rapidly evolving technological landscape, artificial intelligence (AI) and machine learning (ML) have emerged as powerful tools transforming how we live, work, and interact with the world around us. From self-driving cars and personalized health-care to advanced robotics and natural language processing, AI and ML have the potential to revolutionize countless industries and improve the

quality of life for millions of people. However, as with any ground-breaking technology, the development and deployment of AI and ML systems also raise a host of ethical questions and concerns that must be carefully considered by coders, researchers, and policymakers alike.

The importance of ethics in AI and ML development cannot be overstated. As these technologies become increasingly integrated into our daily lives, they have the potential to either reinforce or challenge existing social norms, values, and power structures. By taking a proactive approach to ethical considerations, coders can help ensure that AI and ML systems are designed and implemented fairly, transparently, and beneficial to all members of society.

This chapter will explore some key ethical considerations that coders must consider when working with AI and ML technologies. We will begin by examining the concepts of bias and fairness in AI and ML algorithms, discussing how these issues can arise and what steps can be taken to mitigate their impact. Next, we will delve into the critical topics of privacy and data security, highlighting the importance of safe-guarding user information and maintaining trust in AI systems. We will then focus on transparency and explainability, exploring the need for clear communication and understanding of AI decision-making processes. Finally, we will discuss the role of accountability and regulation in promoting responsible AI development, touching upon the various legal and ethical frameworks emerging to guide the future of AI and ML for coders.

By engaging with these important ethical considerations, coders can play a crucial role in shaping the development of AI and ML technologies in a manner that is both responsible and beneficial to society. As we continue to push the boundaries of what is possible with AI and ML, we must do so with a keen awareness of the ethical implications of our work and a commitment to fostering a more just, equitable, and inclusive future for all.

Understanding Bias and Fairness in AI and ML Algorithms

As we delve into artificial intelligence (AI) and machine learning (ML), coders must understand the importance of addressing bias and ensuring fairness in their algorithms. In this section, we will explore the concept of bias, its impact on AI and ML systems, and the steps developers can take to promote fairness in their work.

Defining Bias in AI and ML

Bias in AI and ML refers to the presence of systematic errors in the algorithms, data, or decision-making processes that lead to unfair or discriminatory outcomes. These biases can stem from various sources, such as the training data, the algorithm's design, or even the developer's unconscious beliefs and assumptions. When left unchecked, biased AI and ML systems can perpetuate and exacerbate existing inequalities, causing harm to individuals and society as a whole.

The Impact of Bias on AI and ML Systems

The consequences of biased AI and ML algorithms can be far-reaching and detrimental. For instance, biased algorithms in hiring processes may discriminate against certain demographic groups, leading to a lack of diversity and perpetuating stereotypes. In facial recognition technology, biased algorithms have been shown to misidentify people of color more than their white counterparts, raising concerns about privacy and civil liberties.

Moreover, biased AI and ML systems can erode public trust in technology as people become increasingly wary of the potential harm these systems can cause. This distrust can hinder the adoption of beneficial AI and ML applications, ultimately stalling progress and innovation.

Promoting Fairness in AI and ML Development

To ensure fairness in AI and ML algorithms, developers must proactively address and mitigate bias. Here are some steps to consider:

- **Curate diverse and representative data:** Ensure that the training data used in developing AI and ML algorithms is diverse and representative of the population it serves. This helps to minimize the risk of biased outcomes and ensures that the system performs fairly across different demographic groups.
- **Regularly evaluate and test for bias:** Continuously monitor and assess AI and ML systems for potential biases during development and after deployment. This can be done through various techniques, such as fairness metrics, bias audits, and third-party evaluations.
- **Encourage interdisciplinary collaboration:** Collaborate with experts from various fields, such as social sciences, ethics, and law, to gain a broader perspective on potential biases and their implications. This interdisciplinary approach can help developers better understand the societal context in which their algorithms operate and make more informed decisions about fairness.
- **Foster a culture of ethical development:** Encourage a culture of ethical AI and ML development within your organization, emphasizing the importance of fairness and the potential consequences of biased algorithms. This can be achieved through training, workshops, and the establishment of ethical guidelines and best practices.
- **Advocate for transparency and openness:** Be transparent about the development process, the data used, and the potential limitations of AI and ML systems. This openness can help build trust with users and stakeholders and facilitate a more informed dialogue about the ethical implications of AI and ML technologies.

In conclusion, understanding and addressing bias in AI and ML algorithms is crucial to responsible development. By taking the necessary steps to promote fairness, developers can create AI and ML systems that are effective and ethical, ensuring a more equitable future for all.

Privacy and Data Security: Safeguarding User Information

As AI and ML technologies advance and become more integrated into our daily lives, the importance of privacy and data security cannot be overstated. In this section, we will explore the significance of safeguarding user information and the steps coders can take to ensure that their AI and ML systems are designed with privacy and data security in mind.

The rapid growth of AI and ML has led to unprecedented data being collected, stored, and analyzed. This data often includes sensitive personal information, such as financial records, health data, and location data. As a result, the potential for misuse or unauthorized access to this information is a significant concern. In addition to the potential harm to individuals, data breaches can lead to significant financial and reputational damage for companies.

To address these concerns, coders must prioritize privacy and data security when developing AI and ML systems. This can be achieved through technical measures, organizational policies, and adherence to relevant regulations and industry standards.

One of the critical technical measures that can be implemented is data anonymization. This involves removing personally identifiable information (PII) from datasets, making it more difficult for individuals to be identified. Data masking, pseudonymization, and aggregation can be used to achieve this goal.

Another critical aspect of data security is encryption. By encrypting data at rest and in transit, coders can help protect sensitive information from unauthorized access. Additionally, implementing strong access controls and authentication mechanisms can reduce the data breach risk.

Organizational policies also play a crucial role in safeguarding user information. Companies should establish precise data collection, storage, and usage guidelines and procedures for handling data breaches. Regular audits and assessments ensure that these policies are followed and that potential vulnerabilities are identified and addressed.

Compliance with relevant regulations and industry standards is another essential aspect of privacy and data security. In many jurisdictions, specific laws govern the collection, storage, and use of personal information, such as the European Union's General Data Protection Regulation (GDPR) and the California Consumer Privacy Act (CCPA). By familiarizing themselves with these regulations and adhering to industry best practices, coders can help ensure their AI and ML systems are legally compliant and secure.

In conclusion, privacy and data security are critical considerations for coders working with AI and ML technologies. By implementing technical measures, establishing organizational policies, and adhering to relevant regulations and industry standards, developers can help safeguard user information and build trust in their AI and ML systems. As the field continues to evolve, coders must remain vigilant and proactive in addressing these concerns, ensuring that AI and ML technologies are developed and deployed responsibly.

Transparency and Explainability: Building Trust in AI Systems

As AI and ML systems become increasingly integrated into our daily lives, developers must prioritize transparency and explainability in their creations. These two factors play a crucial role in building trust between users and AI systems, ensuring that the technology is effective and ethically sound. This section will explore the importance of transparency and explainability in AI and ML development and discuss strategies for achieving these goals.

Transparency refers to the openness and clarity with which an AI system operates. It involves providing users with information about how the system works, the data it uses, and the decision-making processes it employs. This level of openness allows users to understand the rationale behind the AI's actions and decisions, fostering trust and confidence in the technology.

Explainability, on the other hand, refers to the ability of an AI system to provide clear, understandable explanations for its decisions and actions. This is particularly important when AI systems are used in critical decision-making processes, such as medical diagnoses, financial investments, or legal judgments. Users must comprehend the reasoning behind the AI's decisions to trust the technology and feel confident in its capabilities.

To achieve transparency and explainability in AI and ML systems, developers should consider the following strategies:

- **Design with transparency in mind:** From the outset, developers should prioritize transparency in their AI systems. This includes selecting easily interpretable algorithms and designing user interfaces that clearly communicate the system's processes and decision-making rationale.
- **Provide clear documentation:** Comprehensive documentation is essential for transparency and explainability. Developers should create user guides, technical documents, and other resources that explain the AI system's inner workings, data sources, and decision-making processes in an accessible and understandable manner.
- **Implement explainable AI techniques:** Explainable AI (XAI) is an emerging field focusing on developing AI systems that provide clear, human-understandable explanations for their decisions and actions. Developers can improve explainability and foster user trust by incorporating XAI techniques into their AI systems.
- **Engage in open communication:** Developers should be open to feedback and questions from users, regulators, and other stakeholders. By engaging in open communication and addressing concerns, developers can demonstrate their

commitment to transparency and explainability and build trust in their AI systems.

- **Collaborate with ethicists and other experts:** To ensure that AI systems are developed with transparency and explainability, developers should collaborate with ethicists, social scientists, and other experts who can provide valuable insights and guidance on ethical considerations.

In conclusion, transparency and explainability are essential for responsible AI and ML development. By prioritizing these factors and implementing the strategies discussed in this section, developers can build AI systems that are not only effective but also ethically sound, fostering trust and confidence among users. As AI and ML technologies continue to advance, developers must remain committed to these principles, ensuring that the future of AI is both innovative and ethically responsible.

Accountability and Regulation: Ensuring Responsible AI Development

As we delve deeper into artificial intelligence (AI) and machine learning (ML), it becomes increasingly crucial for coders to understand the importance of accountability and regulation in the development process. In this section, we will explore the role of these two factors in ensuring responsible AI development and discuss how coders can contribute to a more ethical AI landscape.

Accountability in AI development refers to the responsibility of developers, organizations, and other stakeholders to ensure that AI systems are designed, implemented, and used in a manner that adheres to ethical principles and guidelines. This includes being answerable for the consequences of AI systems, whether intended or unintended, and taking necessary steps to mitigate any potential harm.

One of the key aspects of accountability is the need for developers to be aware of the potential biases and ethical implications of their AI systems. This involves conducting thorough assessments of AI algorithms and datasets to identify and address potential issues related to fairness, privacy, and transparency. By doing so, developers can ensure that their AI systems are effective and ethically sound.

Regulation, on the other hand, refers to establishing and enforcing rules and guidelines that govern the development and use of AI systems. These regulations are typically set by governments, industry bodies, or other relevant authorities and are designed to ensure that AI development adheres to ethical standards and best practices.

In recent years, there has been a growing call for more robust and comprehensive AI regulations, as concerns about the potential misuse of AI technologies and their impact on society continue to rise. Some key areas where regulation is needed include data privacy, algorithmic fairness, and transparency.

As a coder working in AI and ML, staying informed about the latest developments in AI regulations and guidelines is essential. This helps you ensure that your work complies with the relevant rules and enables you to contribute to the ongoing conversation about responsible AI development.

One way to stay updated on AI regulations is by following the work of organizations and initiatives focusing on AI ethics, such as the AI Ethics Guidelines by the European Commission, the AI Now Institute, and the Partnership on AI. These organizations often publish research, recommendations, and guidelines that can help inform your work and ensure you are responsibly developing AI systems.

In conclusion, accountability and regulation are crucial in ensuring responsible AI development. As a coder working in AI and ML, it is your responsibility to be aware of your work's ethical implications and adhere to the relevant guidelines and regulations. By doing so, you can contribute to developing effective and ethically sound AI systems, paving the way for a more responsible and inclusive AI landscape.

The Future of Ethical AI and ML for Coders

As we conclude this chapter, it is essential to reflect on the critical role that ethics plays in the development of artificial intelligence and machine learning technologies. The rapid advancements in these fields have brought numerous benefits, from automating mundane tasks to revolutionizing industries. However, these advancements also come with a responsibility for coders to ensure that the AI and ML systems they create are ethical, fair, and transparent.

This chapter has explored various ethical considerations, such as understanding bias and fairness, privacy and data security, transparency and explainability, and accountability and regulation. By addressing these concerns, coders can contribute to developing AI and ML systems that are both efficient and morally sound.

The future of ethical AI and ML for coders lies in the continuous pursuit of knowledge and understanding of the ethical implications of their work. As technology evolves, so must the ethical frameworks that guide its development. Coders must remain vigilant about the latest ethical concerns and best practices in AI and ML development.

Moreover, collaboration between coders, ethicists, policymakers, and other stakeholders is crucial in shaping the future of ethical AI and ML. By working together, these groups can develop comprehensive guidelines and regulations that ensure AI and ML technologies are used responsibly and for the betterment of society.

In addition, fostering a culture of ethical awareness within the coding community is vital. This can be achieved through education, mentorship, and sharing resources and experiences. By cultivating an environment where ethical considerations are integral to the development process, coders can ensure that AI and ML technologies are built on a foundation of responsibility and integrity.

Ultimately, the future of ethical AI and ML for coders has immense potential and opportunity. By embracing the ethical considerations outlined in this chapter and committing to responsible development practices, coders can play a pivotal role in shaping a world where AI and ML technologies are used to enhance our lives, promote fairness, and uphold the values that define our humanity.

Chapter Summary

- Ethics in AI and ML development is crucial, as these technologies have the potential to either reinforce or challenge existing social norms, values, and power structures.
- Understanding and addressing bias in AI and ML algorithms is essential for responsible development, ensuring fairness, and avoiding perpetuating inequalities.
- Privacy and data security are critical considerations for coders working with AI and ML technologies, requiring technical measures, organizational policies, and adherence to relevant regulations and industry standards.
- Transparency and explainability are essential components of responsible AI and ML development, fostering trust and confidence among users.
- Accountability in AI development refers to the responsibility of developers, organizations, and other stakeholders to ensure that AI systems adhere to ethical principles and guidelines.
- Regulation is necessary to establish and enforce rules and guidelines that govern the development and use of AI systems, ensuring adherence to ethical standards and best practices.
- Collaboration between coders, ethicists, policymakers, and other stakeholders is crucial in shaping the future of ethical AI and ML, developing comprehensive guidelines and regulations.
- Fostering a culture of ethical awareness within the coding community is vital, achieved through education, mentorship, and sharing resources and experiences, ensuring AI and ML technologies are built on a foundation of responsibility and integrity.

THE FUTURE OF AI AND ML IN CODING AND BEYOND

I n recent years, the world has witnessed a technological revolution that has transformed the way we live, work, and interact with one another. At the forefront of this revolution are artificial intelligence (AI) and machine learning (ML), two rapidly evolving fields that have the potential to revolutionize not only the coding industry but also the very fabric of our society. As we stand on the cusp of a new era, coders, developers, and technology enthusiasts must embrace the AI and ML revolution and harness its power to create a smarter, more efficient world.

This chapter aims to provide a comprehensive overview of the current state of AI and ML in coding and explore the potential implications of these technologies for the future of the industry and beyond. By examining major themes and findings, we will unravel the core insights of AI and ML for coders, highlighting the significance of these advancements in shaping the future of technology and society. Furthermore, we will address the limitations and critiques surrounding AI and ML development, offering recommendations for overcoming these challenges and paving the way for a more sustainable, ethical, and inclusive technological landscape.

As we delve into the world of AI and ML, it is essential to recognize that these technologies are not merely tools for coders to wield; they are powerful forces that have the potential to redefine the way we approach problem-solving, decision-making, and innovation. By embracing the AI and ML revolution, we can unlock new possibilities for growth and development, empowering individuals and organizations to reach new heights of success and efficiency.

In the following sections, we will explore the major themes and findings of AI and ML for coders, discussing the implications and significance of these technologies for the industry's future and beyond. We will also address the limitations and critiques of AI and ML development, offering insights and recommendations for overcoming these challenges and fostering a more sustainable, ethical, and inclusive technological landscape.

As we embark on this journey, let us remember that the future of AI and ML in coding and beyond is not predetermined; it is up to us to shape it. By embracing the AI and ML revolution and harnessing its power for good, we can create a smarter, more efficient, and more connected world than ever before.

Unraveling the Core Insights of AI and ML for Coders

As we delve into artificial intelligence (AI) and machine learning (ML), we must understand the major themes and findings that have emerged in recent years. These insights provide a solid foundation for coders looking to incorporate AI and ML into their work and offer a glimpse into the future of these transformative technologies.

The Power of Data

One of the most significant revelations in AI and ML is the importance of data. Data is the lifeblood of these technologies, as it provides the necessary information for algorithms to learn, adapt, and improve. Coders must recognize the value of collecting, processing and analyzing vast amounts of data to create intelligent systems capable of making informed decisions and predictions.

The Rise of Deep Learning

Deep learning, a subset of ML, has emerged as a game-changer in AI. Deep learning algorithms can process and analyze complex data with remarkable accuracy by utilizing artificial neural networks that mimic the human brain's structure and function. This breakthrough has led to significant advancements in areas such as image and speech recognition, natural language processing, and autonomous vehicles.

The Integration of AI and ML in Various Industries

AI and ML have transcended the boundaries of computer science and are now being integrated into a wide range of industries. These technologies are revolutionizing our lives and work, from healthcare and finance to agriculture and entertainment. Coders must be prepared to adapt their skills and knowledge to meet the demands of an increasingly AI-driven world.

The Ethical Considerations of AI and ML

As AI and ML continue to advance, ethical considerations have come to the forefront of the conversation. Coders, researchers, and policymakers must address issues such as data privacy, algorithmic bias, and the potential loss of jobs due to automation. Understanding and addressing these concerns ensures that AI and ML are developed and implemented responsibly.

The Need for Collaboration and Interdisciplinary Approaches

The development of AI and ML requires a collaborative and interdisciplinary approach, combining elements of computer science, mathematics, psychology, and other fields. Coders must be willing to work with experts from various disciplines to create innovative solutions that push the boundaries of what is possible with AI and ML.

In conclusion, understanding these major themes and findings is crucial for coders harnessing AI and ML's power. By embracing the importance of data, deep learning, industry integration, ethical considerations, and interdisciplinary collaboration, coders can play a vital role in shaping the future of technology and society. As we continue to explore the potential of AI and ML, the possibilities are limitless, and the impact on our world will be profound.

Shaping the Future of Technology and Society

As we delve into the third chapter of our conclusion, it is crucial to understand the far-reaching implications and significance of artificial intelligence (AI) and machine learning (ML) in coding and beyond. The transformative power of these technologies has the potential to reshape not only the way we develop software and applications but also the very fabric of our society. In this section, we will explore the various ways AI and ML are poised to revolutionize the world of technology and the broader implications for our society.

First and foremost, the integration of AI and ML into coding practices will lead to a significant increase in efficiency and productivity. By automating repetitive tasks and streamlining complex processes, developers can focus on more creative and innovative aspects of their work. This, in turn, will lead to the creation of more advanced and sophisticated software capable of solving problems and addressing challenges that were once considered impossible.

Moreover, adopting AI and ML in coding will result in more personalized and user-centric applications. As these technologies become more adept at understanding and predicting user behavior, developers will be able to create software that caters to individual users' unique needs and preferences. This will enhance the overall user experience and foster a more inclusive and accessible digital landscape.

However, the implications of AI and ML extend far beyond coding. As these technologies continue to advance and permeate various sectors, we expect to see a profound impact on the job market and the economy at large. While some fear that the rise of AI and ML will lead to widespread job displacement, others argue that these technologies will give rise to new industries and employment opportunities. In either case, governments, businesses, and educational institutions must adapt and prepare for the inevitable changes the AI and ML revolution brings.

Furthermore, integrating AI and ML into our daily lives will also have significant ethical and societal implications. As we become increasingly reliant on these technologies, privacy, security, and accountability questions will become more pressing. It is crucial for stakeholders to engage in open and honest dialogue about the potential risks and benefits of AI and ML and to establish guidelines and regulations that ensure these technologies' responsible and equitable development.

In conclusion, the implications and significance of AI and ML in coding and beyond are vast and far-reaching. As we embrace the AI and ML revolution, we must remain cognizant of the potential challenges and concerns accompanying these advancements. By fostering a culture of innovation, collaboration, and responsibility, we can harness the power of AI and ML to shape a brighter, more efficient, and more inclusive future for all.

Addressing the Challenges and Concerns in AI and ML Development

As we delve into the fascinating world of artificial intelligence (AI) and machine learning (ML), we must acknowledge the limitations and critiques accompanying these groundbreaking technologies. By addressing the challenges and concerns in AI and ML development, we can better understand the potential risks and work towards creating a more responsible and ethical future for these technologies.

Data Quality and Bias

One of the most significant challenges in AI and ML development is ensuring the data quality used to train algorithms. Data is the lifeblood of AI and ML systems, and the quality of the data directly impacts the performance and accuracy of these systems. Poor data quality can lead to biased or inaccurate results, which can have severe consequences in real-world applications.

Moreover, AI and ML systems are susceptible to biases in the data used to train them. These biases can result from human prejudices, cultural norms, or systemic issues. Developers need to be aware of potential biases and work towards creating more diverse and representative datasets to minimize the risk of perpetuating harmful stereotypes or discrimination.

Security and Privacy Concerns

As AI and ML technologies become more integrated into our daily lives, concerns about security and privacy have become increasingly prevalent. The vast amounts of data collected and processed by AI and ML systems can pose significant risks if improperly protected. Developers must prioritize data security and privacy, ensuring that sensitive information is not compromised or misused.

Additionally, the rise of deepfake technology, which uses AI and ML to create realistic but fake images and videos, has raised concerns about the potential for misinformation and manipulation. Addressing these concerns requires a combination of technological advancements, legal frameworks, and public awareness to mitigate the risks associated with deepfakes and other AI-generated content.

Ethical Considerations

The development of AI and ML technologies raises numerous ethical questions, such as the potential for job displacement, the impact on human decision-making, and the responsibility for AI-generated outcomes. As AI and ML systems become more autonomous, it is crucial to establish ethical guidelines and frameworks to ensure that these technologies are developed and deployed responsibly.

Developers, policymakers, and society must engage in ongoing discussions about the ethical implications of AI and ML, striving to strike a balance between innovation and the potential consequences of these technologies.

Technical Limitations

Despite the impressive advancements in AI and ML, technical limitations still hinder their full potential. For instance, AI and ML systems often require vast computational power and energy, which can be costly and environmentally unsustainable. Additionally, many AI and ML algorithms struggle with understanding context and nuance, which can lead to misinterpretations or incorrect conclusions.

Addressing these technical limitations requires continued research and development and collaboration between academia, industry, and government to drive innovation and overcome these challenges.

In conclusion, while AI and ML technologies hold immense promise for revolutionizing the world of coding and beyond, addressing the limitations and critiques accompanying these advancements is essential. Acknowledging and addressing these challenges, we can work towards a more responsible, ethical, and sustainable future for AI and ML technologies.

Paving the Way for a Smarter, More Efficient World

As we conclude our exploration into the world of artificial intelligence (AI) and machine learning (ML) for coders, it is essential to reflect on the transformative potential of these technologies. Integrating AI and ML into the coding landscape has already begun to revolutionize how we approach problem-solving, decision-making, and the development of innovative solutions. In this final section, we will summarize our key findings and offer recommendations for harnessing the power of AI and ML to create a smarter, more efficient world.

Throughout this book, we have delved into the intricacies of AI and ML, examining their applications, benefits, and challenges. We have seen how these technologies can enhance the capabilities of coders, enabling them to create more sophisticated and intelligent software systems. By automating repetitive tasks, optimizing algorithms, and facilitating the analysis of vast amounts of data, AI and ML can significantly improve the efficiency and effectiveness of coding processes.

However, integrating AI and ML into the coding sphere is challenging, as with any technological revolution. Concerns surrounding data privacy, security, and ethical considerations must be addressed to ensure the responsible development and deployment of these technologies. Additionally, the potential for job displacement and the need for upskilling and reskilling in the workforce must be considered as AI and ML continue to advance.

With these considerations in mind, we offer the following recommendations for paving the way toward a smarter, more efficient world:

- **Encourage collaboration and knowledge-sharing:**
  Fostering a culture of collaboration and knowledge-sharing among coders, researchers, and industry professionals will be crucial in driving innovation and overcoming the challenges associated with AI and ML. By working together, we can develop best practices, share resources, and create a strong foundation for the responsible growth of these technologies.
- **Invest in education and training:** As AI and ML continue to reshape the coding landscape, investing in education and training programs is essential to equip coders with the skills and knowledge necessary to thrive in this new era. This includes not only technical skills but also a strong understanding of the ethical and societal implications of AI and ML.
- **Develop ethical guidelines and regulations:** To ensure the responsible development and deployment of AI and ML, it is crucial to establish ethical guidelines and regulations that govern their use. This will help to address concerns surrounding data privacy, security, and the potential for bias and discrimination in AI-driven systems.

- **Promote transparency and accountability:** Encouraging transparency and accountability in developing and deploying AI and ML systems will be essential in building trust and fostering responsible innovation. This includes communicating the capabilities and limitations of AI-driven systems and ensuring that developers and organizations are held accountable for their actions.
- **Embrace a human-centric approach:** As we continue integrating AI and ML into the coding sphere, it is essential to remember the importance of maintaining a human-centric approach. By prioritizing human values, needs, and experiences, we can ensure that these technologies are used to enhance our lives and create a more equitable, inclusive, and sustainable future.

In conclusion, the future of AI and ML in coding and beyond holds immense promise and potential. By embracing the AI and ML revolution and addressing its challenges and concerns, we can pave the way for a smarter, more efficient world that benefits all of humanity. The journey has only just begun, and the possibilities are truly limitless.

ABOUT THE AUTHOR

Andrew Hinton is a prolific author specializing in Artificial Intelligence (AI). With a background in computer science and a passion for making complex concepts accessible, Andrew has dedicated his career to educating others about the rapidly evolving world of AI. His debut series, AI Fundamentals, is a comprehensive guide for those seeking to understand and apply AI in various professional settings. Andrew's work caters to a broad audience, from managers to coders, breaking down AI basics, essential math, machine learning, and generative AI clearly and engagingly. His ability to demystify the complexities of AI has made him a trusted voice in the tech industry. Andrew's work imparts knowledge and empowers his readers to navigate and innovate in an AI-driven world.

$10.99 FREE EBOOK

Receive Your Free Copy of The Power of AI

SCAN ME

Or visit:
bookboundstudios.wixsite.com/andrew-hinton